PENGUIN BOOKS

REAL COOKING

'No one else writes more sensually or simply about food ... this food bubbles, splatters, hisses and crackles on the page and causes the reader to salivate and start cooking immediately ... with stuff of this quality around, it's just possible that the Great British Public knows when it's on to a good thing' Rowley Leigh, *Guardian* Weekend

'Nigel ia a real lick-the-spoon sort of cook ... He positively makes you want to cook his effortlessly simple dishes – such as bacon and chicory gratin, or spiced lentils with cream and ginger ... *real cooking* is a book destined to become stained and smeared through over-use' Lindsey Bareham, *Evening Standard*

Slater concentrates on simple, unfussy dishes and comfort food. But it is the way he lovingly describes the food that makes his books so enticing' *GQ*

'The sort of book you'll get lovingly smeary with greasy fingerprints and drops of oil' Nigella Lawson, *Vogue*

'*Real Cooking* written in the author's practical, down-to-earth and witty style is a must for all cooks, regardless of skill. Roast Pork with Rosemary and Garlic and Split Pea Soup with Moroccan Spiced Butter are just two of the deliciously "do-able" recipes' *Women & Home*

'The hallmark of Nigel Slater's style is great-tasting no-fuss food – and never more so than in his new book *Real Cooking*' Sarah Stacey, *Marie Claire*

ABOUT THE AUTHOR

Nigel Slater is the author of *Real Fast Food* (1992), *Real Fast Puddings* (1993), *The 30-minute cook* (1994), *Real Good Food* (1995), *Real Cooking* (1997) and *Nigel Slater's Real Food* (1998) which won a Glenfiddich award. *Real Fast Food* was shortlisted for the André Simon award, *The 30-minute Cook* was nominated for both the Glenfiddich and Julia Child awards. In 1995 he won the Glenfiddich Trophy and he has twice won the cookery Writer of the Year award (1995 and 1999), as well as being named Media Personality of the year in the 1996 Good Food Awards. He is Food Correspondent of the *Observer* and writes a monthly column for *Sainsbury's Magazine*.

ABOUT THE PHOTOGRAPHER

Georgia Glynn Smith Trained at St Martin's School of Art and worked as a designer in London and New York before turning to photography. Her passion for food, plants, people and gardens has led to numerous commisions and off-beat assignments. Her work appears regularly in the *Independant*, the *Guardian*, *Elle Decoration* and *Gardens Illustrated*. This is her first food book.

REAL COOKING

Nigel Slater

Photographs by Georgia Glynn Smith

PENGUIN BOOKS

PENGUIN BOOKS

Published by the Penguin Group
Penguin Books Ltd, 80 Strand, London WC2R 0RL, England
Penguin Putnam Inc., 375 Hudson Street, New York, New York 10014, USA
Penguin Books Australia Ltd, Ringwood, Victoria, Australia
Penguin Books Canada Ltd, 10 Alcorn Avenue, Toronto, Ontario, Canada M4V 3B2
Penguin Books India (P) Ltd, 11 Community Centre, Panchsheel Park,
New Delhi – 110 017, India
Penguin Books (NZ) Ltd, Cnr Rosedale and Airborne Roads,
Albany, Auckland, New Zealand
Penguin Books (South Africa) (Pty) Ltd, 24 Sturdee Avenue,
Rosebank 2196, South Africa

Penguin Books Ltd, Registered Offices: 80 Strand, London WC2R 0RL, England

www.penguin.com

First published by Michael Joseph 1997
Published in Penguin Books 1999
21

Set in Monotype Baskerville
Designed in QuarkXpress on an Apple Macintosh
Printed and bound in China by Hung Hing

There is too much talk of cooking being an art or a science –
we are only making ourselves something to eat.

Contents

For Digger, Magrath and Poppy – as always

Acknowledgements

My thanks to Louise Haines, my editor at Michael Joseph, whose idea it was that I should write in the first place; her boundless enthusiasm, clear thinking, support and patience are more than an author could ever wish for. My thanks too go to Eleo Gordon and everyone at Michael Joseph and Penguin, especially Christabel Gairdner, Caz Hildebrand and Andrew Barker.

Thank you to my agents Araminta Whitley at Lucas, Alexander and Whitley and Rosemary Scoular at Peters, Fraser and Dunlop; to Justine Picardie and everyone at *The Observer*; to Robert Breckman; and to Chris Rodriguez and Richard Partin for their help. I particularly want to thank Georgia Glynn Smith for her wonderful photographs. And to Delia and Michael with love.

The photographs

The photographs for *Real Cooking* were taken by Georgia Glynn Smith. They are unusual in that they are totally natural – not set up or contrived in the typical way of food photographs – Georgia simply followed me around my home kitchen taking her photographs while I cooked. This is why you see the same pans and plates throughout the book, rather than the usual hired tablesettings and props, with plates and linen chosen by a stylist to match the food. This 'natural', warts-and-all way seemed more appropriate to the book. (Of course, we have got rid of most of the pictures I didn't want you to see – like the ones of the cat deciding to help himself to a piece of fish in the middle of a recipe or the mess I sometimes get in when I'm cooking.) We have tried to make every picture tell you something about the recipe, focusing on a small but important point without actually turning it into a step-by-step cookery course. Having said that, some of the pictures are there for no other reason than to encourage you to have a go yourself. That is the whole point of the book.

Introduction

I passionately believe that anyone can make themselves something good to eat. Cooking is a whole lot easier than many people think. Good cooking – real cooking – is within the grasp of anyone with an appetite and a few pots and pans. There is nothing difficult about it (it is only supper after all), so we can pretty much ignore all that stuff about it being 'an art', 'a science' or 'a gift'.

It takes no expertise to heat some butter and a squashed clove of garlic in a shallow pan till it froths and bubbles, then slide in a piece of chicken. Let it cook till its skin is crisp and golden, then squeeze in half a lemon and serve it with its pan juices and a leafy salad to mop them up. Anyone can slap a lamb chop on a hot grill pan, throw a handful of pasta into bubbling water or put an apple to bake in a hot oven. I work from the not unreasonable premise that if someone can make a cup of coffee then they can probably roast themselves a chicken.

Real cooking is not about making fancy stocks and sauces, piping purées and perfecting spun-sugar baskets. Real cooking is about making ourselves something to eat that involves a bit of simple roasting, grilling or frying. Nothing complicated. Nothing that is not within the grasp of a novice cook. But it is cooking, rather than opening a packet or a tin. As you will see, real cooking is also about the little things – the small points that turn such straightforward cooking into good cooking. The attention to detail that makes a simple supper into something sublime.

What makes something really good to eat? What is the difference between cooking something that is merely fuel and something that is a joy to devour? It is certainly not the need to make our cooking more complicated, neither is it an art that we must have at our fingertips. It is simply the understanding of the little things that make something especially good; the golden, savoury goo that builds up under a pork chop you have left to cook slowly in its pan; the intense flavour of the bits of lamb that have caught on the bars of the grill; the gravy that you make from the sticky bits left in the pan after you have sautéed some chicken thighs. This is real cooking. The roast potato that sticks to the roasting tin; the croûton from the salad that has soaked up the mustardy dressing; the underneath of the crust of a blackberry and apple pie, rich with purple juice; these are the things that make something worth eating. And worth cooking.

I am not sure that anyone needs to learn how to make *mosaique de poulet sauce gibiers*, but how to roast a chicken so that its skin is crisp and its flesh juicy is certainly worth knowing. And knowing, too, that the best bits of all are the treasures hiding under the roast bird – those gloriously gooey, chewy bits that others miss. Small things matter. Such as learn-  ing when to leave alone. The piece of fish, pork or lamb left to bubble in its pan without being fiddled with will form a delectably sticky, savoury crust; one that is stirred and tinkered with won't.

The recipes in this book are straightforward, with a friendly, familiar ring to them. There are no outlandish combinations or flash presenta- tions. These are recipes that warm, satisfy and please. Because for the most part this is what I believe we want from our food. Some of the recipes are new, such as Thai pork rissoles with lime and mint or grilled mack- erel with sherry vinegar, while others walk in like an old friend, say tarragon chicken or old-fashioned fish cakes.

You will notice that the recipes use a mixture of definite

weights, e.g. 500g, and more relaxed measures such as 'a fistful'. This is quite deliberate. I feel it is easier for a cook, particularly an inexperienced one, to start with an exact weight of the main ingredient, e.g. 2 pork chops, about 350g each; but then the recipe loosens up a little, allowing cooks to use their instinct and

tastebuds rather than blindly follow a recipe as if it were carved in stone. Where measurements are crucial, in mixing polenta for instance, then I tell you. Where quantities can be more relaxed, then I leave it up to you (a handful, a pinch or two). I mean, do you know anyone who actually weighs the spinach for a salad?

Late last year my phone rang with an enquiry about a recipe. Could I tell the caller whether the 2 tablespoons of chopped parsley were level or heaped? I was exasperated. What, I thought, have we done to our cooking? We have turned the joy of making something to eat into something approaching a chemistry lesson. As cookery writers, we risk holding the reader's hand too tightly, thus destroying the trust that they should have in their own judgement. In these recipes I hope I have given enough detail for the inexperienced cook while at the same time making it clear that there is more to cooking than following an idiot-proof formula minute by minute, gram by gram.

Yes, we all want recipes that work, but it is foolish to treat them as gospel. There are too many variables – the state of the ingredients, the size and weight of your pans, the accuracy of your oven and the power of your hob – for cooking to depend purely on following a recipe. We need to apply a soupçon of common sense, too. Blindly following a recipe as if it were a chemical formula is not really cooking, it is just going through the motions.

I will tell you something else; in this sort of basic, no-messing home cooking (as opposed to the beautifully honed recipes of starred chefs) quantities are often not *that* critical. Here I often refer to a handful of something rather than an accurate quantity because I have found a bit more or less makes little difference, and is something that can be left to the taste or whim of the cook. In other words, a gram or two either way makes bugger-all difference. We are not chefs chasing Michelin stars here – we are simply making ourselves something to eat.

Pots, Pans & Heat

We don't need a load of fancy equipment just to make ourselves something to eat. A couple of strong, heavy pans and a sharp knife that fits your hand is worth all the gadgets and gismos in the world. But that doesn't mean that we are going to get out of this cheaply.

With pans, pots and knives you tend to get what you pay for. Those offers for mega-sets of enamelled saucepans that you see in those wretched little magazines which fall out of the Sunday papers are not worth the paper they are printed on. Thin and weak, they will bend and burn and their handles will work loose in a few months. You will do better to spend the money on just one strong, heavy pan.

A good pan makes all the difference to our cooking. By good I mean one that is heavy and has a thick base, so that it stays flat and does not buckle or get little pits in it. A pan with a solid bottom is less likely to burn our supper.

For someone who spends their life cooking I have surprisingly few pots and pans. When I bought them I seriously questioned my sanity. How could anyone in their right mind spend so much on so few saucepans? Yet here they are, fifteen years on, as good as new. Used pretty much every day, on the hob, in the oven, in and out of the dishwasher, yet they are as sturdy as the day I bought them. They cook evenly and slowly. Steady but sure.

In other words go for broke. I recommend solid stainless steel pans. Stir a sauce with a metal spoon in an aluminium pan and the sauce will turn grey. Something tells me this cannot be  a good thing. Enamelled pans, provided they are the very solid French cast iron variety, are strong and heavy (too heavy for some) but have a tendency to chip. I have a French enamelled cast iron casserole and some baking dishes that have been with me for years. Love them to bits. Heavy though. Cooking with them is better than working out.

I make do with a small 20cm diameter pan, another that is about 25cm and a third that I use for pasta, soups and stews that is about 30cm. These are deep, Italian-made pans with a layer of copper running through the base (to conduct the heat), sandwiched between the stainless steel. The best money I have ever spent. What I particularly like about them is their small handles are made of the same steel, which means they go into the oven as well as on the hob.

I have a couple of deep sauté pans, again stainless steel, that serve as frying pans and are also capable of going in the oven.

They are Swiss and can be found at cookware shops specialising in professional catering equipment. Again, lots of money, but they are much better than the cheaper alternatives whose handles crack and wobble, whose enamel coating peels off and which develop 'hot spots' on the bases. Hot spots where food catches and burns. One of my best buys has been a ridged cast iron grill pan, the sort that sits on the hob and leaves enticing black grill lines on your meat. You will need a good extractor fan, though, as they kick up a lot of smoke.

It is different with knives. I believe that the best knife is the one that you like best. Most of us have a special little knife that seems to work for us – even though it may not be the sharpest and has probably seen better days. So what. That is the best knife you could have. But if you ever have to buy a new set I might suggest you look for a 20cm cook's knife in stainless steel, one where the blade goes right down inside the handle and is securely bolted in. Great for chopping veg, parsley and the like.

Sharpening knives has an element of mystery about it. I have never mastered the technique that well. I recently bought one of those neat little knife sharpeners where you slide the blade between two rollers. They really do work. The trick is to remember to do it regularly, like flossing.

A good pan. A favourite knife. Time to get on with it.

Fish & Shellfish

The less you do to a fish the better it tastes. I believe this passionately. A quick dip in a pan of spluttering butter, held down on a blistering griddle or a quiet bake in the oven is all it needs. Fish hates fuss. I cannot see the point of turning a fillet into a mousse in order to stuff another fillet. I can see even less why that fillet will appear with a sauce made from crushed crayfish and cream. I am not even sure that fish should ever appear in *haute cuisine* to be pummelled and poached, prettied and primped and served with a puff pastry crescent. I would rather fry a fresh fish in a bit of butter and eat it with a squeeze of lemon and a lump of bread.

I hold fish in the highest esteem. It suits my way of eating, my way of life. Fish tantalises (with ginger and lime) and soothes (with tarragon and cream). It satisfies without filling and digests without notice. For me it is the perfect food.

It also stinks (but only if it is not fresh), it also has bones (but only if prepared without care) and it is also expensive (but only if we ignore the cheaper varieties). Nevertheless, its purity of flavour, versatility and ease of preparation make up for any shortcomings. At least in my book they do.

Shellfish, by which I mean mussels, oysters, crabs and the like, is the very essence of the sea. Loud, salty, savoury flavours. Wobbly, creamy, quivering flesh. A reluctance to complicate the issue, with spices, herbs and brutish seasonings, will be rewarded. Though crab can take a dash of mustard and chilli. They all love citrus. Salty fish and a squeeze of lemon are stunning in the mouth.

When shopping for fish and shellfish, the fishmonger's slab should be our starting point, not the shopping list. The fish shop is not the place to go with preconceived ideas – save them for the butcher. Check what's on offer. Be choosy. He won't be choosy whose money he takes. Go for whatever looks the freshest. If it tempts on the slab it will tempt on the plate. Fresh fish should positively shine with health (apart from haddock, which is a dull old bird to look at). The colours should sing, the eyes should sparkle and the flesh should be wet and slippery. Look into its eyes; they should be clear and bright, begging you to buy.

Supermarket fish and shellfish, encased in plastic and donning a parsley sprig, are worth looking at, though they can rarely hold a candle to the stuff on the wet fish counter. Ask your fishmonger to do anything you don't want to. That's what he's there for. He will scale. He will gut. He will fillet. Just don't ask him to bone your sardines for you. And don't forget to bring something home for the cat.

The white fish

Sole, especially the prized whole Dover, is crisp white tablecloths, doddery waiters and careful, old-fashioned cooking. Sole is toothsome white flesh, soothing and undemanding to eat. Unless you strike a bone. But this is the most delicate of all fish, and it needs our respect.

Sole is a thin fish, almost as thin as plaice. But it is fine fish, too. So let's treat it that way. A hot pan of frothing butter, a squeeze of lemon and, perhaps, a handful of chopped herbs. Not for me the time-honoured sauces of the classical French kitchen. Such flour-thickened masks have nothing to offer the sole or the plaice. Gunge, in the form of traditional white sauces thinned with cream and scattered with sweet grapes, should be kept well away. Gunge in the form of a little pile of buttery mashed potato is another matter altogether. Particularly if it sits next to a stack of limp, dark green beans.

But there is more to white fish than the majestic sole and the slippery, delicate, subtle, spotty plaice. The cod family, lean, sweet and large flaked, offers the cook a chance to play without losing the flavour and texture of the fish. A creamy fish pie, hot Thai citrus fish cakes or old-fashioned English ones with a lovely crust and parsley sauce. A lump of cod thick as a plank, with snow-white flakes as big as your thumb, makes a splendid roast. All it needs is a drizzle of olive oil before it meets the heat, and a wodge of mayonnaise so thick that it stands to attention on the plate.

Skate is the most succulent of fish. No doubt due to the gelatinous nature of its flesh. The ridged white meat of the wings (all white and pink like those of an angel) is textured like no other, falling neatly apart into long, juicy strips. Its unusually meaty flesh responds best to a brief poaching, and accompanied by a buttery sauce. The classical finish of butter browned in the pan and given tartness with a few fat capers is sublime, though a simple butter sauce such as Hollandaise, is as flattering to its luscious flesh as béarnaise is to a beef steak.

Of course, there are others, and I am the first to encourage a little experimentation. I just wish sea bass would come down in price. Dense, delicate flesh with silver and grey markings; the sort of fish an architect might design. A favourite of contemporary chefs, sea bass responds well to roasting or grilling, less so to wet cooking. John Dory, sad looking but a joy to eat, pops up from time to time and should be pounced upon. If you can cope with its grimace.

The oily fish

By oily I mean salmon, mackerel, sardines, herring of course, and those you rarely see at the fishmonger's, such as the darling, delectable little anchovy. Hot from the grill, their skin crisps and blackens, sealing the flavour and juices into the rich, fatty flesh. Their smell, though appetising in the extreme when cooking, can linger like a cigar in a lift. Yet a mackerel singing on the bars of a barbecue is one of the great smells of all time.

For the most part cheap and cheerful, it is the oily fish that offer the richest eating. Some might say too rich. With the exception of salmon, I cannot recommend a cream sauce here. And even for salmon it needs cutting with lemon juice or wine. Something piquant, sharp and citrus is far more adept at bringing out their best.

These are the fishes that shine on the slab. Twinkling blue, black and silver in the ice. But be warned; oily fish must be spanking fresh – eyes bright, colours singing – if they are to be worth eating.

Grilling is my first choice. A raw presentation – the flesh 'cooked' in lemon or lime juice or vinegar – my second. An early job as a kitchen apprentice had me cleaning mackerel for marinating in vinegar, coriander seed and dill. I smelled of fish for weeks, and was befriended by the restaurant cat. A startling starter when served with a dollop of soured cream. The mackerel that is, not the cat. Now my temptation is to fry the fillets, before giving them a brief bath of olive oil, lime and chillies.

Salmon is the king of fish. Certainly it looks pretty in pink, with its cucumber ruff around its neck, but it is its flavour that sells it. Or is this fish's popularity due more to its colour and price? I doubt it is the texture, which inclines towards the woolly. Which brings me to the farmed versus wild dispute, on which I will, for once, hold my tongue.

Trout is another matter. Long gone are the days when trout titillated the palate. Trout is now the battery chicken of the fishmonger's slab. Cheap, satisfying and ubiquitous. That said, trout is the most useful of fish, and is consistently good natured. It will take Indian or Thai spices, and seems to be universally liked – rather like chicken.

And lastly a tiddler. To many, the anchovy is the salt on our pizza. My fishmonger sometimes has a box of fresh anchovies, though I am unsure I want to take them home to stuff them. Life is too short to bone an anchovy. Though the thought of them with Parmesan cheese, hot from the grill, is a thought almost too savoury to bear.

A fish on the grill – or more than likely under it

Sand between the toes and salt on the lips are the best accompaniment to grilled fish. Once we cook fish away from the sea a little magic is lost. But if we are after something for supper rather than the meal of our lives we can invest in little pink and yellow mullet, small enough for two apiece, or a prawn or two that change from grey to orange pink as they cook. To be torn apart by salty fingers in search of juicy flesh. A bigger fish is a splendid treat but hardly practical in today's little kitchens.

The point of grilling fish is to cook it quickly while adding interesting smoky notes at the same time. The skin and scales will form a crisp crust that protects the moist flesh inside. This charred and salty skin peels off to reveal moist flakes of fish. I like a morsel of it now and again just for its intense, smoky, fish flavour. Though it is the very devil to swallow.

The secret to producing a grilled fish worth eating lies as much in harnessing the heat of the grill as it does in careful timing. If the pan is too hot the skin will burn – the fish will dry. If the pan is too cool the juices will leak out. A fierce heat to start with – lowering the heat slightly once the fish is on the grill – seems to me the most reliable way. It is worth remembering that we have only to turn the flesh from translucent to opaque.

I have no doubt that grilled fish is most flavoursome when cooked over charcoal, but in my house this is a rare treat. As this is above all a practical book I shall not assume that a charcoal grill is to hand. What I will assume is that you are prepared to arm yourself with one of those ridged cast iron grill pans I bang on about in the pots and pans section. The one you skipped over.

But what if we are blessed with only a domestic overhead grill? Can we still have grilled fish for tea? Of course we can, and what is more, the fish cooks so quickly that the result can be positively juicy. And that is what matters. But it will lack the smoky punch of food cooked against the hot iron bars of a grill or griddle. Cooked under a hot grill, about 10cm away from the heat, a fish fillet such as trout is cooked in three minutes.

Grilled fish with lime leaves

A punchy version using a griddle or ridged grill pan that sits on the hob, or, at a push, a frying pan. Fresh lime leaves are available from the major supermarkets and from oriental food shops. They freeze well.

Lay the fillets of fish (which shouldn't incidentally be too thick, trout is ideal) on a tray or flat dish. Crush the garlic to a paste with a half teaspoon of sea salt flakes. A pestle and mortar is good for this. A wooden spoon and a bowl is another possibility. Mash in the chopped chilli and the finely chopped lime leaves (roll the leaves up tightly and shred them with a sharp knife, then chop them as fine as tea leaves). Add the lime juice and the oil. Stir and mash it all together.

Spread the resulting paste over the fish fillets. Heat the griddle (or ridged cast iron pan) or grill. It must be really quite hot. Slap the fish skin-side down on the hot grill pan. Press it down with a fish slice or palette knife. Cook until it is charred in ridges, about two minutes. Carefully turn it over (go easy if you don't want to end up with kedgeree) and press the flesh side down. Expect much crackle and smoke. Cook for a minute, maybe two. It is done when the fish is almost opaque. I like it just this side of raw in the middle. Lift off with a fish slice and eat straight away.

The fish could be accompanied by a few leaves of salad and perhaps some new potatoes, or even rice. Though not much.

Per person:

a filleted trout, or tail-end fillets of salmon, haddock or sole, (about 175–200g each)

a clove of garlic, peeled

a small red chilli, seeded and finely chopped

4 lime leaves

juice of half a lime

a tablespoon of olive oil

Grilled mackerel with sherry vinegar

For 2

4 large fillets of mackerel

a thick slice of soft butter, about 50g

2 tablespoons sherry vinegar

Use any mellow vinegar; sherry is ideal, or a really good red wine one perhaps. You can use some of the fancier 'designer' ones if you have that sort of thing. The rougher, cheaper ones are a bit too punchy for this.

Put the fish skin-side down in a grill pan, one suitable for overhead grilling. Lining the pan with foil will make it easier on the washer-up. It will probably be you anyway. Spread the butter on the fish and season it generously with salt and black pepper. Put the fish under a pre-heated grill, about 10cm from the heat source. Grill for about four minutes. Drizzle over the sherry vinegar and spoon any buttery juices from the pan back over the fish. Return to the grill and cook for a couple of minutes until the fish is juicy, smoky and sizzling. Eat with bread and a salad.

Cod, leek and parsley pie

For 6

750ml milk

750g haddock or cod fillet

3 medium-sized leeks, or 2 thick ones

a thick slice of butter, about 50g

250g medium-sized brown mushrooms

a big bunch of parsley, chopped

plain flour, a little

8 anchovy fillets, chopped

3 small gherkins, chopped

12 capers, rinsed

250g cooked, peeled prawns

4 tablespoons crème fraîche (optional)

400g chilled ready-made puff pastry

a little milk or beaten egg for glazing

There is nothing worse than turning up at someone's house for supper to find that they have done something fancy. No one *really* wants *ravioli de fruits de mer aux trois sauces*. We want a big fish pie – a proper one with creamy sauce, lots of chopped parsley and crumbly puff pastry. Oh, and we want peas too – a big dish of them.

You will also need a deep pie dish, with a rim, about 1.5 litres. You can pick them up quite cheaply at old-fashioned ironmongers.

Put the milk in a pan large enough to hold the fish. Put it over a moderate heat and when it starts to shudder and little bubbles come to the surface, slide in the fish. Continue to bring to the boil, then just as the milk starts to rise, turn the heat down (you will have to keep an eye on it up to this point), then leave the fish to simmer gently until it is tender and the flakes come easily apart – a matter of only six or seven minutes. Remove the fish, keeping the cooking liquor (but discarding any skin and bones), and let the fish fall into a bowl in big flakes and chunks.

Meanwhile, trim and slice the leeks into rounds about as thick as your finger, then rinse them thoroughly under running water. Melt the butter in a pan and cook the leeks till bright green and soft. (I know everyone tells you not to use the green bits but just ignore them, it's all good stuff if the leeks are reasonably young.)

This will take a good twenty minutes, so slice the mushrooms while the leeks are cooking. When the leeks are soft add the sliced mushrooms and half the parsley. Cook for about five minutes, stirring from time to time, until the mushrooms are cooked, sprinkle over a little flour (about 3 tablespoons) and cook for a minute then stir in the reserved fishy milk. Bring slowly to the boil, stirring. When the consistency is that of a thick sauce, toss in the anchovies, gherkins and capers and leave to simmer gently, with a generous seasoning of salt and pepper, for about fifteen minutes. Then very gently fold in the fish, the prawns, the rest of the parsley and the crème fraîche if you fancy an especially creamy filling. Check the seasoning. Take care not to smash the flakes of fish.

Spoon into the pie dish. The filling should come almost to the top. Pop something in the middle to hold up the pastry, a cup or an egg cup will do, unless, of course, you have a pie funnel. Let the mixture cool before you attempt to put the pastry on top.

Roll out the pastry to fit the top of the dish – it should be slightly larger than the pie – then wet the rim with water or a little milk. Cut a strip off the edge of the pastry, and press it firmly on to the rim of the dish. Wet the rim of pastry and lay the remaining pastry on top. Press firmly down on the rim, and pinch the edges together to seal. Brush with a little beaten egg, or milk, and bake in a preheated oven at 200°C/400°F/Gas 6 until the pastry is golden brown and crisp at the edges.

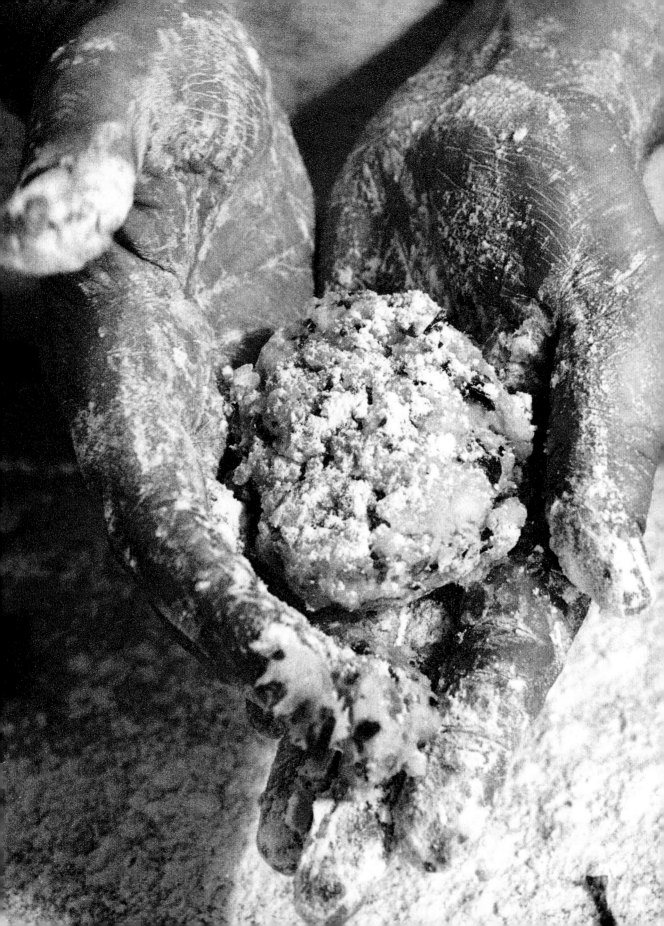

Old-fashioned fish cakes
with creamed spinach

Soothing, pleasing, comforting fish cakes. Traditional recipes contain eggs to bind the fish and spuds and a coating of breadcrumbs. I am not sure they need either. Handled carefully in the pan they won't break up, and the flour forms a delicate golden crust, just like that of a potato cake. The result is delicate, fluffier and somewhat less like the impenetrable commercial versions. They will take an hour – start to finish.

Cut the potatoes into chunks, put them in a saucepan and cover with water. Bring to the boil, add a teaspoon of salt, turn down the heat and simmer till tender, about twenty-five minutes. While they are cooking, put the fish in a shallow pan, almost cover with milk and cook at a gentle bubble until the fish turns opaque and can be pulled apart in big fat flakes. A matter of eight to ten minutes.

Put the chopped parsley, and it should not be too finely chopped, in a mixing bowl. Chop the anchovy fillets and add half of them to the parsley. Lift the fish out of the milk with a slotted spoon and add to the bowl. Break the flakes up gently, removing any bones as you go and taking care not to smash the fish up too much. Season with salt and black pepper.

The spuds should be done by now. Test them with a skewer. Drain them and mash them with the butter. Mix the mash lightly with the seasoned fish. There should be large flakes of fish and flecks of green in the potato. Shape into eight flat cakes by patting them gently in your hand. Don't overdo this or they will lose their rough texture. Pat them in seasoned flour, turning them over to cover both sides.

Heat a little oil in a frying pan. A non-stick one might be the best bet. When it starts to shimmer, add the floured fish cakes. Cook for two minutes on each side, turning them carefully with a palette knife.

Wash the spinach and tear it into small shreds. Put the wet leaves into a shallow pan with the remaining anchovies and cover with a lid. Cook for a minute or two until the leaves have wilted but are still a vivid emerald green. Pour in the cream, add a little salt and some black pepper. Leave to bubble for a couple of minutes. Serve at the side of the fish cakes, with quarters of lemon.

For 4

500g/4 medium-sized potatoes, peeled

500g cod, hake or haddock (or pretty much anything else for that matter), skinned

milk, about 250ml

a large fistful of parsley leaves, chopped

12 anchovy fillets, rinsed

30g butter

flour (enough to cover a plate), seasoned with salt and cayenne pepper

oil

2 big handfuls of baby spinach leaves

150ml double cream or crème fraîche

a lemon

Haddock fish cakes with lime leaves and dipping sauce

For 2

a shallot, chopped

2 cloves of garlic, crushed

2 small hot red chillies, seeded and chopped

a handful of coriander leaves, roughly chopped

6 large lime leaves, shredded

a tablespoon of Thai fish sauce (nam pla)

450g haddock, skinned and chopped (all bones removed)

a little flour

groundnut oil for frying

For the dipping sauce:

6 tablespoons rice vinegar

4 tablespoons sugar

a tablespoon of dark soy sauce

2 small red chillies, seeded and very finely chopped

a tablespoon of coriander leaves, very finely chopped

juice of a lime

A lively mouthful of citrus-flavoured fish cakes with a hot, sweet sauce in which to dip them. I know the ingredients list is long, but the recipe itself is absurdly easy. There is nothing much here you can't get from a really good supermarket. If lime leaves defeat you, lemon grass, shredded very finely, is an admirable replacement.

Put the shallot, garlic, chillies and coriander leaves in the bowl of a food processor and whiz them to a coarse sludge. Add the shredded lime leaves and the fish sauce. Mix to a loose paste.

Tip into a bowl and season with salt. Whiz the fish to a rough paste (don't overdo it), add it to the spice paste and mush the whole lot together. Shape the mixture into about eight round, flat patties with the aid of a little flour to stop them sticking to your hands. Set aside for half an hour for the flavours to mix.

Make the dipping sauce: heat the vinegar and sugar in a small saucepan until the sugar has dissolved and the mixture is becoming syrupy. Stir in the soy sauce and leave to cool. Add the chillies, the coriander leaves and the lime juice.

Heat the oil in a shallow pan. Just enough in which to shallow fry the fish cakes. When the oil is hot, fry the little cakes, a few at a time, until golden, about four or five minutes on each side, maybe a little less. Serve them hot from the pan with the dipping sauce.

A baked fish

In Greece, at least on the islands I have been to, they bake whole fish in round metal tins, seasoned with nothing but olive oil and a few sprigs of thyme. Sometimes there are potatoes, roughly sliced or haphazardly chopped in the same tin. The result is a tender fish that slides effortlessly from the bone. It smells savoury and very slightly burned (which is actually the herbs), the flesh and skin split open in patches as if it has been stabbed. The look is primitive, as old as time, and the taste, when eaten with fresh bread and slightly too much cold wine or beer, is sublime.

I see no reason to gild this lily, even though its rusticity may seem out of place in a state-of-the-art English kitchen. It is the kitchen that is wrong, not the fish. If I do make any additions it will be little more than a few cloves of garlic, squashed so they cook as quick as the fish, or perhaps a few stalks of dill or slices of lemon. Chunks would be more in keeping. If the fish is white, then a green herb, perhaps tarragon or fennel, or some spices if the fish is up to it – mackerel or cod for instance.

A lazy but frugal and intelligent practice is to throw the potatoes and vegetables into the tin as well. They might as well cook while the oven is on. Perhaps some halved tomatoes with a little salt, oil and crushed basil leaves, or a handful of beans, green ones, to wilt a little in the hot oil. The Greeks have a way of baking fish in this manner that seems to result in a moist fish no matter how long they leave it in the oven or on the warming plate. I don't know how they manage to do this. It must be their ovens. Five minutes too long in mine and I have got burnt offerings. I often refer to a baked fish as a roast one, the word roast being more instantly appealing to me.

Roast fish with Indian spices and coconut

For 2

a small palmful/a tablespoon of
coriander seeds

5 good pinches/a teaspoon of
cayenne pepper

6 black peppercorns, coarsely
ground

4 or 5 good pinches/a teaspoon
of ground turmeric

3 pinches of ground cinnamon

2 spring onions, chopped

a lump of creamed coconut (about
50g)

2 large fish fillets (about 225g
each) or fish steaks or cutlets

a little melted butter and lime
juice to serve

Fragrant rather than hot. A suitable method for fillets of mackerel, and fillets or steaks of cod, hake, haddock or some of the more unusual whole fish.

Set the oven at 200°C/400°F/Gas 6. Toast the coriander seeds in a small pan over a moderate heat until golden, then crush to a powder using a coffee grinder or pestle and mortar. Mash all the spices together with the spring onions, creamed coconut and a little salt. Spread this moist, crumbly paste on top of the fish steaks or fillets, then bake until the fish is just opaque and thoroughly hot and the topping fragrant. It will not brown or move much. Depending on whether you bought fillets or steaks, this will take anything from ten to twenty minutes. A thick fillet of trout will take twelve. Pour over a little melted butter and a squeeze of lime juice as you serve.

Roast fish with lemon and mint

For 2

2 large fillets of fish (any fish will
do), about 225g

oil – any sort

a small shallot or spring onion,
very finely chopped

a small handful of mint leaves

2 small chillies, seeded and finely
chopped

juice of a lemon or lime

extra virgin olive oil

Roast the fish – high temperature, high speed – then dress it with a sour, bright mixture of citrus and herbs. A highly flavoured olive oil for the dressing will make the whole dish sing.

Put the fish fillets in a roasting tin and drizzle with a little oil and a scattering of salt. Roast in a hot oven (220°C/425°F/Gas 7) until the flesh has turned opaque and is hot right through. About ten minutes. (A thick fillet of haddock or cod will take about twelve to fifteen.) Meanwhile, whiz the onion, mint, chillies and lemon or lime juice together with enough olive oil to make a wet slush. When the fish comes out of the oven, piping hot, pour over the dressing and eat straight away.

Greek baked fish

Heat enough olive oil in a shallow roasting tin to cover the bottom generously. Add the wedges of potato, onion and the garlic and cook them over a moderate heat. After ten minutes or less they will be soft and lightly coloured. Put them in an oven preheated to 180°C/350°F/Gas 4 for ten minutes. Shake them about a bit, then put the fish on top of them and surround with the tomatoes. Add the herbs, the lemon juice and some salt and coarsely ground pepper. Bake for thirty-five minutes. Five minutes one way or the other will make little difference. If you need to, you can keep the dish warm for a while without it drying up by covering it with a lid and keeping it in a very low oven. It comes to no harm when the Greeks do it.

For 2

olive oil

8 small potatoes, wiped and cut into wedges lengthways (in half, then half again)

a medium-sized onion, roughly sliced

2 large, juicy cloves of garlic, peeled and sliced

a medium-sized whole fish or 2 large white fish steaks (cod, haddock, hake, sea bass, monkfish, mackerel etc.), about 225g each

4 tomatoes, halved

oregano, mint or dill – a handful of chopped leaves

juice of a large lemon

Roast cod

For 2

olive oil

butter, a thick slice

cod fillet, 2 x thick 200g slices, as thick as you can get it, skin on

Fat flakes of juicy fish – golden on top, pearly white underneath. Here's how. You'll probably want some buttery mash (page 249), a panful of buttered spinach, and a huge, quivering dollop of garlic mayo (page 48) too. Or perhaps a dollop of the salsa verde on the facing page.

Preheat the oven to 200°C/400°F/Gas 6. Put a little olive oil – just a couple of good glugs – in a frying or roasting pan. It will be going in the oven so make sure it has a metal handle. Melt the butter in the oil till it froths and bubbles. Season the fish with salt and black pepper. Put the fish, skin side down, into the frothing butter and oil. Let it cook at a lively pace for a minute or so till the skin is golden brown, then turn it over and transfer to the oven. Roast for about eight minutes, or until the fish is opaque right through. Put it back for a few minutes longer if it is not cooked through.

Salsa verde

A loud, creamy, tart sauce that goes with, frankly, anything. If you haven't a food processor or blender then chop everything by hand and beat in the oil with a whisk. Almost better than Tom Ketch. It will keep for a couple of days in the fridge.

Chuck everything but the oil and lemon juice into the food processor. Whiz till blended, then slowly pour in the olive oil until the mixture is a rough, creamy, piquant sludge. Smarten the flavour with a little lemon juice, salt and black pepper. Ready.

For 4–6

a large bunch of parsley, stalks
   removed
6 bushy sprigs of mint
a large handful of basil leaves
2 cloves of garlic, crushed
a tablespoon or so of Dijon
   mustard
8 anchovy fillets, rinsed
3 tablespoons capers, rinsed
6 tablespoons extra virgin olive oil
2 tablespoons lemon juice

A fish in the pan

A fresh fish, dusted with flour and dipped into a pan of foaming butter, cannot be beaten in the simple-supper stakes. The flour forms a light and appetising crust while keeping the flesh moist within. Try it with sole, plaice or any flat fish. Try it with trout, John Dory or any fish steak.

A handful of chopped parsley and the wringing out of a lemon over the pan at the end of cooking are the only embellishments necessary. Though a knob of fresh butter, added to the pan after the fish is on the plate but before the herb goes in, would appeal. To ring the changes, throw in a few capers, rinsed of their brine, some chopped bacon or a shake of the Tabasco bottle. But only if it is right for the fish.

Flour is not the only provider of crust and protector of flesh; cornmeal, yellow and coarsely ground, will give a crisp coating (though watch it does not burn) and oatmeal can be used in the Scottish manner with oily, full-flavoured fish.

A pan-fried fish

For 1
a lump of butter, about 50g in
    weight
a fish, whole or filleted
milk
flour
a little bit more butter to finish
lemon

Melt the butter in a shallow pan over a moderate heat. Dip the fish, which can be a sole, a plaice, a mullet or fillets of almost anything, into a little milk (just enough to wet the surface), then into flour. You can season the flour with salt and a little finely ground black pepper if you wish, or season the fish as it cooks. When the butter foams and froths, add the fish or fillets. Leave untouched until the underside is golden, a matter of about three minutes, while the butter bubbles around it. Turn the heat down if the butter looks as if it may burn. With a fish slice, turn the fish over. Cook until the second side is golden, then check for doneness by sliding a flake of fish out with a small knife. If it is tender and opaque it is done. Cook it no further.

Lift the fish on to a warm plate, then tip out the butter. Add a new lump of butter, nothing much – about the size of a walnut in its shell – to the pan, then heat it till it begins to froth. When it turns golden brown, a matter of a minute or so, pour it, still fizzling, over the fish and eat immediately, with a good squeeze of lemon juice.

Sole with butter and green herbs (and, if you wish, a little cream)

Sole is a mighty fine fish that comes at a mighty fine price. A sole on my plate is a bit of a treat, so it is given the simplest of treatments – hot pan, a little butter and some herbs. Nothing more.

Heat the butter in a large shallow pan over a medium heat. It will start to froth with lots of small bubbles. Dust the fillets lightly with flour. Place them in the butter and cook until they start to colour. A minute or so. You may need to do this in two batches. Then carefully turn them using a palette knife and your finger, flipping them over in the butter to cook on the other side.

Almost at once throw the chopped parsley and sorrel leaves into the pan. If you are using spinach add a little lemon juice, too. When the underside of the fish is golden, season with a little salt and shake the pan about a bit to mix the herbs and the butter. Remove the fish and pour the sauce over. That's it really.

If you fancy a rich sauce then add a drop of cream, as much as you like but no more than three or four tablespoons. French beans, cooked till floppy, and perhaps some new potatoes, tiny ones in their skins, would suffice as accompaniment.

For 2
a lump of butter (about the size of a golf ball)
4 large fillets of sole
flour
chopped parsley – a handful
a few leaves of sorrel (or baby spinach), rolled up tightly and shredded
lemon juice
cream (but only if you wish)

Pan-fried plaice with lemon and parsley butter

For 2
2 good-sized, spanking-fresh
    plaice
flour
butter, about 50g
a handful of parsley, chopped
the juice of a lemon, unless it is
    large, then use half

A mild and gentle supper. Some green beans would be nice here. New potatoes, too. Very, very small ones. Get them ready first, the fish only takes a few minutes.

The plaice should be slippery and wet. If they are not, then dip them in a little milk. Dust them with flour. Melt most of the butter, about two-thirds, in a large shallow pan until it froths and bubbles. Slide in the plaice (you may have to do one fish, then the other). You will see it shrink a little in the pan. The bubbles should frame the fish. Cook till golden underneath, about one minute. Turn carefully and cook for a further two. If the butter browns, turn the heat down. The fish should be golden brown on top, the flesh white and wobbly underneath. Lift out on to hot plates. (If you are cooking them in relays then you may need to add a second knob of butter for the other fish.)

Tip out the butter. Put in the remaining fresh butter, then let it froth and turn golden brown. But only just. Throw in the parsley and squeeze in the lemon juice. Cook for thirty seconds. Pour the contents of the pan over the fish and eat immediately, while it sizzles.

A refreshing salsa for a pan-fried fish

Serves 2–3
a small red onion, finely diced
6 ripe, sweet summer tomatoes
2 small red chillies, seeded and
    finely sliced
a good handful of coriander
    leaves, chopped
juice of 2 limes
caster sugar
fruity olive oil

A crude, raw sauce for serving with fish and chicken.

Put the diced onion in a bowl. Chop the tomatoes into small dice removing only their hard cores. I disagree with those who say you should skin, core and seed a tomato for salsa. What's left? A blob of red slush – that's what. Anyway, put the tomatoes in with the onion and the chillies. Gently mix in the coriander leaves, lime juice and a knife-point of sugar. Add salt, erring on the side of generosity. Drizzle with a little olive oil and serve shortly after making – before the coriander goes black.

Salmon with sherry vinegar and capers

Melt half the butter in a shallow pan over a medium heat. As soon as it starts to froth add the salmon fillets. Skin side down. Cook until the skin starts to turn golden brown and crisp, about three minutes, then carefully turn them over. The heat should not be too high at this point. After two minutes the flesh will be cooked right through and caught golden brown in patches. Lift the fish carefully out on to a warm plate and throw away the butter in the pan – it has done its job and will burn if you cook it any longer.

Wipe the pan out with kitchen paper. Add the remaining piece of butter and leave it until it froths. Watch it carefully while it turns golden, nutty brown. I might add that at this point it burns easily. One minute nut-brown butter, the next acrid black oil. When the butter is deep gold, pour in the vinegar. It will hiss back at you. Then toss in the capers and parsley. Just warm the capers through (their flavour bullies if they get hot), shaking the pan about a bit, then pour the vinegar and caper sauce over the salmon. A little salad, crisp and green, would be nice.

For 2

butter – about 100g

2 pieces of salmon fillet, about 150g each

4 tablespoons sherry vinegar

a tablespoon of capers, rinsed

a small handful of chopped parsley

Pan-fried Thai fish

Mackerel, salmon, cod or haddock will be fine here.

Mix the lime juice, fish sauce, sugar, chopped chillies, lemon grass, lime leaves and ginger. Warm the oil in a shallow pan. When it sizzles, add the spice mixture and the fish. Cook for a minute or two until the fish is golden, then turn and cook the other side. A flat metal slice will make things easier.

Remove the fish from the pan, add three shakes of soy sauce and four shakes of rice wine. Big, bold shakes. Then pour over the bubbling juices from the pan. Serve hot, perhaps with a little rice.

For 2

juice of 2 limes

a tablespoon of Thai fish sauce (nam pla)

a little sugar, about a teaspoonful

2 small red chillies, seeded and finely chopped

a stalk of lemon grass, shredded

6 lime leaves, shredded

a lump of ginger about as large as a walnut, peeled and shredded

2 tablespoons groundnut oil

2 pieces of fish, about 200g each

soy sauce

rice wine

A day on the slab

My fishmonger is a third-generation fishmonger. He is helpful, friendly and full of gossip about the fish trade. There is a whiff of arrogance about him that I like. An arrogance that comes from running a shop that is a model of freshness and variety that other fishmongers would do well to copy. His shop, more of a stall really, is in North London among a row of tawdry wine bars and shops selling second-hand fridges. To those in search of a piscine supper it is a little Mecca and is, to my mind, the best fish shop in London.

There are scallops on the shell, quivering with delight, a wooden box of oysters snapped tightly shut, and a bag of mussels, all blue shells and barnacles. Tiny mussels too, no bigger than a thumb nail, loose on the ice. I have come in for herrings but they are dull today. A pile of plaice from Brixham catches my eye. Small and delicate white kites of plaice, all slippery and tempting.

There are little red mullet, pink and tight and firm. There is as much bone and fin as flesh, but what there is is all meaty and crumbly, and smells of the sea. A fish for the grill. There are prawns, some plump and grey, some pink and out of a packet.

There is a graphic fan of skate wings for frying with parsley and capers or poaching with lime and coriander.

Then there is salmon, both farmed and wild. Both cutlets and fillets. There is a small fish for cooking whole and a bigger one for a wedding. But if salmon wasn't pink, would we get such a choice? There is sole for the rich, and lemon sole for me. One of the soldierly row of crabs would make a lovely tea with brown bread and butter and mayonnaise. Under the table there is a box of black and blue lobsters, straitjacketed with green rubber bands. I feel sorry for them and look away.

To my left are three boxes, one of squid, all white and shiny. They will cook in seconds on the grill, with hardly time to dress the salad. Look! There are blue and steel sardines for grilling and a floppy octopus peeping over the edge. I see hunks of cod for roasting and there's even fish flaps for the cat.

So why are there fish fingers again for tea?

Poaching fish

Poaching is the gentlest of cooking methods, lulling the fish into tasting good. Exactly the opposite of grilling with all its fire and brimstone. Cooking a fish in water seems an appropriate end, and it is particularly suited to the meaty cuts and whole fish – especially for those that are to be served cold.

Poaching is not boiling. If you boil a fish you end up with soup. Cloudy soup. Poaching is a delicate method that involves immersing the fish in barely moving water. There should be just the occasional blip and shudder from the water, rather than the steam and furious bubbling you get in boiling.

The firmer the fish the better. In other words salmon rather than plaice. The poaching liquid can be water. Or milk. Or water and milk. It can be salted or not, or seasoned with sweet vegetables and herbs; onions, carrots, parsley and pepper. Though I am not sure that it makes that much difference. Water with a bit of sea salt in it seems to do the trick.

Poached haddock
with parsley, cream and dill

For 2

2 pieces of haddock, cod or other white fish, about 175g each
milk, about 175ml
6 tablespoons crème fraîche
butter, a small piece about the size of a walnut
a good handful of parsley, chopped
a handful/about 3 tablespoons chopped dill

Rich, unctuous, soothing.

Put the fish in a shallow pan and pour over enough milk almost to cover it. Bring the milk up to a simmer and cook at a gentle bubble until the flesh of the fish turns opaque and a flake comes away easily when pulled – about eight to ten minutes, depending on the thickness of your fish – turning once.

Lift the fish out with a fish slice to a warm plate. Stir the crème fraîche into the milk (there won't be much left) and continue to simmer for a couple of minutes. You will see it start to thicken. Whisk in the butter, parsley and dill and season with a little black pepper and some salt. Allow to bubble for a minute, then pour over the fish. Serve with mashed potatoes.

Poached salmon

Come high summer, there is little more useful than a piece of cooked salmon in the fridge. You can hack off a lump for lunch, or slide an elegant wedge off the bone for supper. You can serve it with a dithering dollop of mayonnaise or a variation of; perhaps with chopped green things in it, watercress and the like.

The best method I have come across for cooking a large piece of salmon without drying it out is the simplest. It is not my idea, but has been used for some time. It works. It is effortless. And here it is again. (Oh, and anyone who tells you that cooking a salmon should be done in a court bouillon, the stock with onions, carrots and herbs, is having you on. Use salted water instead, it makes not the slightest bit of difference.)

Wash the salmon and check that the fishmonger has removed all the scales and the blood inside. He probably won't have. Even though you told him to. Put the fish into a large deep pan. I use my roasting tin because it is quite deep. Others swear by a fish kettle. I once had one, but ended up planting hyacinths in it. They were a lovely show. Pour enough water over the fish to cover it. Use a measuring jug so you know how much you have used. Add salt to the ratio of 50g of salt per litre of water. It should taste stronger than seawater but slightly less salty than an emetic.

Bring the fish slowly to the boil. It will take a while, then watch it carefully. There should be little more than a bubble or two before you turn off the heat. Clap on the lid, one that fits tight. Leave overnight to cool. The result will be a moist, but not wet, fish. Lift out of the water, which you might as well throw away as it is too salty for stock, and carefully peel the skin off the fish. All you need now is some sauce to go with it. How about some quivering mayonnaise as glossy as a tart on a Saturday night?

For 4–6
a large piece of salmon on the
   bone, just over 1kg in weight
salt

Fish soup

People make such a fuss about fish soup. All that careful timing, fiddling preparation and elaborate assemblies. What is better to my mind is a clear, simple soup made with only a couple of fish and flavoured in an uncluttered way with, say, tarragon or lime.

Fish soup was once the food of the poor fisherman. Not so now. A hearty soup rich with fish and shellfish will cost us dear, and tends to fall into the special-occasion category. Of course, the cost depends on which fish we choose. There is plenty of flavour in the cheaper fish; coley, haddock and mussels, for instance. But they are not always exciting on the plate. Fish soup needs something for the eye as well as the mouth. A little red mullet to add colour and meaty flesh, a handful of prawns to tear apart with fishy fingers, or even a scallop or two. But it is a mistake to let fish soup get too complicated.

First stop – the fishmonger's. I think we are better off without the oily, fatty fish such as mackerel and salmon. Their boisterous flavour tends to overpower everything else. White fish and something flash to go on top are all we need. I tend to buy only two sorts of fish and two of shellfish. I don't like playing guess-the-flavour and prefer to go for a simple soup rather than the show-off's version.

Fish soup needs a little sweet veg in it; fennel perhaps, a little onion and possibly some herbs (tarragon is wonderful, so is dill). A few chopped tomatoes will add freshness. But the real joy of fish soup is that there is no definitive recipe. There are no clever-clogs purists waiting to hiss at our ideas.

I am a fan of the broth-like soups with lumps of fish and shellfish in them rather than the thick purée type. Though creamy shellfish soups such as crab are another thing altogether. I suppose they could be loosely called a stew. I like my fish soups to resemble a romanticised fisherman's quayside cooking pot rather than a plate of piscine glue.

A French(ish) fish broth

A clear, mildly flavoured broth in which the fish keep their individual flavours. It is not cheap to make but will feed four. The garlic mayonnaise and floating toast are, I think, essential.

Put the onion and leeks in a deep stainless steel pan with enough olive oil to cover the bottom of the pan. Cook them over a moderate heat until they soften. They should not colour, just turn translucent and tender. A matter of five to seven minutes. Add the celery, garlic and fennel, cook for a minute or so then add the potatoes. Stir and add the Pernod, saffron and dried chilli and cook for about ten minutes until the potatoes start to soften. Then add salt and enough boiling water to come a good way over the contents – about 1 litre should do it.

   Let the mixture simmer gently for about ten minutes. Cut the fish into large chunks, then when the potatoes are tender to the point of a knife add the white fish, the tomatoes and the tarragon. Continue cooking until the fish has become opaque, then add the mullet and the shellfish. Simmer for a further couple of minutes, skimming off any froth, before turning off the heat as soon as the mussels have opened.

   Divide the vegetables and fish between four soup plates or bowls. Taste the broth, add salt and a little black pepper and, if you think it needs it, a squeeze of lemon juice. An extra splash of Pernod (just a splash) would not go amiss. Pour the broth over the fish and serve with toasted crusts and garlic mayo (see next page).

For 4

a medium-sized sweet onion, quartered
3 small leeks, sliced and rinsed
mild olive oil
3 small stalks of celery, chopped
6 plump cloves of garlic, squashed
a small fennel bulb, thinly sliced
2 medium-sized potatoes, cut into chunks
a tablespoon of Pernod
a big pinch of saffron threads
a big pinch of chilli flakes
about 750g fish (say, haddock or monkfish, red mullet, 8 scallops and a handful of mussels)
4 medium-sized tomatoes, chopped
a good handful of tarragon leaves, chopped
bread, garlic mayonnaise to accompany

Bits to float in your soup

Fish soup isn't fish soup without its traditional accompaniments bobbing around in it. Sinking the mayonnaise-topped croûtes into the liquid with your spoon is part of the fun. A grown-up's version of sinking your rubber duck in the bath. To be honest, the crisp toasted baguette slices and dollops of potent mayo will turn the most unexciting of broths into something worth eating. But I had better not say they are the best bits.

a few thin slices of baguette, toasted
a bowl of garlic mayonnaise (recipe page 48)
grated Gruyère cheese

Garlic mayonnaise

Enough for 4

At room temperature:
2 egg yolks
2 plump, fresh cloves of garlic,
   crushed
300ml fruity olive oil
a little lemon juice

Garlic-scented mayonnaise can be as slapdash or as time-consuming as you wish to make it. A few crushed cloves stirred into a jar of ready-made mayonnaise is a bit of a cop-out but better than no garlic mayo at all. Home-made aïoli, on the other hand, is a magical paste worth every second of pounding and beating. Up to you.

Put the egg yolks either in a mortar or the bowl of an electric mixer. Add the crushed garlic and beat well with a pinch or two of salt. Pour the olive oil in a slow, steady trickle, beating all the time. As it thickens you can be a little more rash in pouring in the oil. Purists, aesthetes and those who don't like washing up will use a pestle and mortar, though the mayonnaise works perfectly well in the mixer. The consistency should resemble thick and glossy mayonnaise. Season with a little lemon juice, salt and finely ground pepper. It will keep in a screw-top jar in the fridge for several days.

Prawns

Forget the frozen ones. They are fine in a prawn cocktail, lost in tender lettuce and pretty pink mayonnaise, but offer nothing for the cook. Go for fresh – they will be grey rather than pink – and cook them the day you buy. They deteriorate faster than you can say smell. I might add that ready-cooked prawns in their shell can be pretty good anyway.

Prawns with lemon butter

Soften the butter in a small saucepan till warm and almost liquid. Stir in the lemon juice. Stop if there seems too much, lemons can be very juicy sometimes.

    Grill the prawns, lightly rinsed, at a high heat for two minutes on each side. You will need to do this six at a time, unless you are barbecuing them in the garden. It may not seem like long, but prawns overcook in the blink of an eye. Pile them on to a warm plate. Put the plate on the table, letting everyone jump in, peeling off the prawns' crisp armour and dipping each into the warm, lemony butter.

Enough butter for 2–4 servings
butter (about 100g)
juice of 2 lemons
prawns, lots, big and fat (you will need about 6 per person)

Grilled prawns and garlic mayonnaise

Summer's day, pile of prawns, pot of garlic mayonnaise. Bliss, yes. But even better if the sun is high, the prawns are hot from the grill, their shells still crackling, and the mayonnaise is heavily laden with garlic. Peel the hot, slightly blackened shells away with your fingers and dip the pink flesh into the garlic mayo. You will get in a mess, of course, but at least it will be a delicious mess. Fingers that taste of grilled seafood and garlic are the best tasting fingers of all. Well, *almost*.

    If smelling like a French cat is not your thing, then you can buy ready-cooked, peeled prawns and toss them in the mayonnaise, with lots of chopped, bright green parsley, then scoop them up on to fingers of brown toast. A nice enough summer lunch or snack, but, I think, somehow rather missing the point.

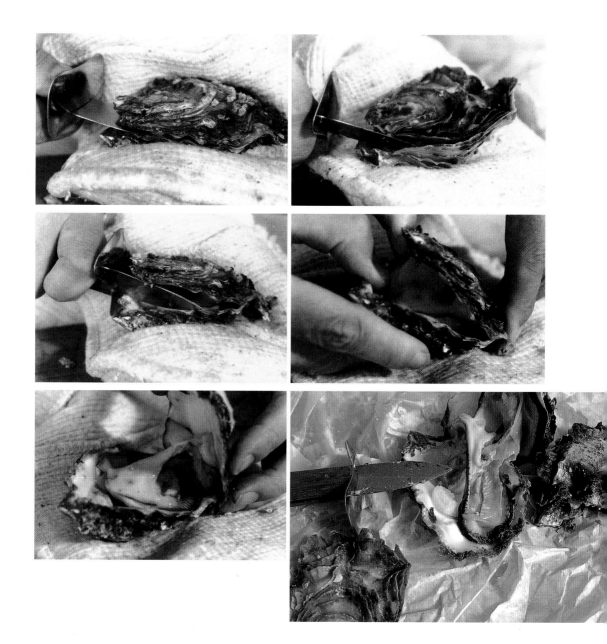

Oysters

No food beckons in quite the same way as an oyster on its open shell. Ridiculously sexy, salty, juicy, quivering things that they are. Yet the oyster does not appeal to everyone, possibly because of its association with smart city restaurants where they are consumed out of bravado as much as for flavour.

Only the wasteful, the crusty and the frigid take them down in one gulp. Suck, gulp, gone. What a waste. Chewing an oyster, even slightly, releases the salty, fishy tang. And then it slides down.

So what is the oyster doing in a book that encourages us to cook? Quite simply, because an oyster is just as good to eat once cooked. It is just different. Those who get snooty about cooking oysters are missing some good food. Dropped wet, wobbly and lightly floured into a pan of shallow, frothing butter, they are done in a minute. Maybe less. The alarm bell sounds when their edges start to curl. They will be lightly crisp outside (eat them quickly before they soften), their insides all trembling, creamy flesh. As seductive a mouthful as it is possible to imagine.

I did not know I liked oysters until quite recently. I only knew I ought to like them. I bought three, ready opened, in Paris – which seemed an appropriate place to lose my virginity – and smuggled them up to my hotel room. Like an adolescent with a tart. One swallow and I was hooked.

Oyster soup is good, too. More of a stew with all those lumps. Cream in this instance does not dilute the flavour, only adding voluptuousness. In the States, where such things are taken very seriously, war will rage over the authentic recipe. My version, as you may have come to expect by now, is slightly unorthodox. Even so, it makes the point. Salty, creamy and fishy. As if you have stirred cream into the sea.

To open an oyster you need to break the hinge that holds the shells together. Not the easiest job if you don't do it regularly. Hold the oyster flat in a well-protected hand – a good thick oven glove will do – then push a short, strong knife in between the shells at the thin end. Wiggle the blade till the hinge breaks, then twist firmly, levering apart the shells as in the pictures opposite.

Creamed oyster toasts

For 2

a lump of butter, about 30g

a shallot, finely diced

6 oysters, pulled from their shells,
    juices kept

2 tablespoons white wine

100ml double cream

Tabasco

paprika

parsley, a palmful, chopped

2 rounds of hot toast to serve

Melt the butter in a shallow, heavy pan. Add the shallot and fry it, gently bubbling in the butter until it is translucent. A matter of five minutes. Pour the juices from the oysters into the shallots. Do this through a tea-strainer so that no shrapnel from the shells gets in, then pour in the wine. Season lightly with a very little salt and some black pepper. Pour in the cream.

Bring the mixture almost to the boil. Drop in the oysters and cook in the gently bubbling cream until their edges start to curl invitingly, a minute or two only. Stir in a good few shakes of Tabasco and a couple of pinches of paprika. Throw in the parsley. As soon as the mixture is really hot then pour over the toast and eat immediately.

Fried oysters

For 2

8 oysters, removed from their
    shells

flour

butter

lemon

Tabasco

A little Tabasco will accentuate the oysters' nautical flavour. Too much will kill it.

Dust the oysters very lightly with flour. I said lightly. Melt a little butter in a shallow pan, just enough to cover the bottom. When the butter starts to sizzle drop in the oysters, one by one. The butter should be hot enough to splutter a bit. Cook the oysters for about one minute without moving them, then turn and cook the other side. They should be golden in patches.

Scoop them out on to a hot plate, then add a little more butter to the pan; a lump about the size of a whole walnut will do. When it sizzles, add a few good squeezes of lemon juice and a shake of the Tabasco bottle. About six shakes actually. Pour the hot, lemon-chilli juices over the oysters and eat with lots of crusty bread to mop them up. Green salad on the side would be good, too.

Grilled oysters with tarragon garlic butter

If you think you might not like oysters, then try them this way.

Mash the butter with the garlic, shallots and tarragon leaves, then stir in the lemon juice. Place the opened oysters in a grill pan. A deep layer of salt or dried beans will keep them from rolling over and spilling their load. Spread dollops of the flavoured butter over the oysters, then dust quite thickly with breadcrumbs. But not so thickly as to cover completely the butter that buries the oysters.

Cook them under a hot grill till the butter starts to bubble and the crumbs brown a little. They should be done in about five minutes.

For 2
150g butter
a plump and juicy clove of garlic,
    finely chopped
2 shallots, finely chopped
a handful of tarragon leaves,
    chopped if large
juice of half a lemon
12 oysters, opened
a handful/about 6 tablespoons
    fresh breadcrumbs

Squid

My fishmonger often has a box of white, tentacled squid. All spooky, wet and dithering. Druids in the rain. Even a fearless cook may find them daunting. There is much juice, some of it black, some of it smelly. Ink and stink. Rather in his shop than my bag. The fishmonger or one of his boys will do the dirty work – removing ink sacs and other yuk. I just pay up for an oven-ready squid, ending up with neat white rings and clusters of tentacles. Rubber bands and bunches of legs. Unless I ask him to open the fish out flat, so that it eats like a thin, white steak.

In Greece I have often watched the island boys, all suntans and wet shorts, battering the sad, ghostly things against the rocks to tenderise them. I am not sure the baby ones, barely 10cm long, need it. They batter them again, this time in flour and milk, before frying them in hot oil till they sing and splutter. About thirty seconds.

I like fried squid. Good for the jaws. I like it best when I am on holiday. Salt on my lips, lemon juice on my squid. Like cabbage, squid needs to be cooked for thirty seconds or thirty minutes, but rarely in between. If you have bought a slab of squid – its body sac opened out like a book – it will benefit from tenderising. Of course you can bash it against the rocks, though a little cross-hatching with a very sharp knife might be more appropriate. Cook it for seconds, though even then do not expect it to melt in the mouth. That is not really the point.

Slap it into a hot cast iron grill pan, one with deep ridges, and press it down hard. It will squeak, its cut edges blackening here and there, turning a boring piece of white muscle into a tantalising mouthful of scorched fish, lemon and salt.

Tiny squid, by which I mean less than 7.5cm long, are sweet and tender and need nothing more than slapping on the grill, then anointing with a squeeze of lime and sprinkling of rough salt. Peel off their mauve-freckled gossamer skin before you cook if you wish. Just find an end and pull. Though it is bound to tear and shrivel in the heat anyway.

Grilled squid with tomato onion salsa

A dazzling plate: white, black, orange, green and red. Get the fish-monger to do all the yukky stuff for you. All you want to know about is a parcel of fresh, clean squid ready to slap on the grill.

Make the salsa first; the squid will be cooked before you can say cephalopod. Peel, stone and dice the avocado neatly. Don't maul it, you will end up with slush. Mix all the salsa ingredients gently together.

Heat the grill pan. One of those ridged cast iron ones is best (unless, of course, you have got the barbecue out). Slap the squid on the hot grill. It will sizzle and hiss at you. Press it down on the pan. One minute. Turn it over. Another minute. Lift it off, sprinkle over a little salt and put it on to a warm plate with the salsa. Be quick – it's going cold. Drizzle over some olive oil, squirt lots of lemon juice over it, scatter with salt and the chopped chilli. Now eat the hot, salty, smoky squid. Quickly, while it's still piping hot.

For 2

12 baby squid or 450g of larger
   squid, prepared
extra virgin olive oil
lemon
a medium-sized red chilli, very
   finely chopped

For the salsa:

a medium avocado, ripe but firm
a handful of small tomatoes, about
   10, chopped
half a small red onion, finely
   chopped
a small red chilli, finely chopped
a palmful of coriander leaves,
   chopped

Crab

The most savoury of seafood. The most juicy, too. Of course, crab is really a seaside treat to be eaten within a cockle's throw of the pier, but a treat that can taste almost as good at home. Just close your eyes and think of Cromer.

A freshly cooked crab can seem like the food of the gods, wrenched limb from limb on the kitchen table for Saturday tea. Chips of cream and orange shell all over the show. Best fun for those with the time to dismantle a freshly cooked crab are the spindly, hairy legs – precious little meat but such sweet juice. You may need to improvise with tools from kitchen, workbench and sewing kit. Such a task should not be hurried. You cannot hurry a crab tea. And neither should you.

I shall not suggest you dress a crab unless you have time to kill. With nothing else to do it can be a fun thing – cracking, wrenching, smashing, picking, pulling and gouging. Not to mention licking your fingers and sucking bits of shell. But there is an alternative for the short of time – and I am not talking about those crab sticks, the long white digits that have never even seen the inside of a crab.

Fishmongers and many major supermarkets often sell neat dressed crab all ready to scoff. It is not as dear a way to buy as you might think, especially if time is money to you. Such a neat little package – everything done and, what is more, they often still include the crab's toes to suck.

There are good reasons for cooking a crab, too. Both the white (juicy) and orange-brown (savoury) meat. Those who scorn the brown meat don't know what they are talking about. For the cook there is crab soup, rich and voluptuous, crab cakes, to be served crackling from the pan, and baked crab, the richest food known to man. Tip the meat into a basin, scooping out from the shell any bits the fishmonger has missed, mix in a few capers, some mustard, a shake of Tabasco, a squeeze of lemon and a few fresh breadcrumbs. Put it in a shallow dish, then scatter it with Parmesan cheese and a dribble of cream. Grill or bake till bubbling and hot. A salad, crisp in the extreme, is the accompaniment you will crave. Try curly frisée leaves and grapefruit – an old-fashioned yellow one if you can find such a thing. Oh, and some watercress, lush green and lots of it.

A little piquancy works wonders with this particular shellfish, either in the form of mustard and capers or lemon (juice or grass) or lime (juice or leaves). The crab loves chilli too – in the form of cayenne in the American-style patties (below) or substitute crab for the haddock in the Thai-style fish cakes on page 32.

Crab cakes

American-style crab patties, rich and filling. Handle them carefully, lifting them in and out of the pan with a fish slice.

Mix together all the ingredients except the oil and season with salt and pepper. Leave in the fridge for at least twenty minutes. With heavily floured hands, gently (and I mean gently) shape the mixture into nine round patties. The less you handle them the easier the job will be. As you shape each one, put it on to a floured plate.

    Heat a little groundnut oil in a frying pan – just enough to cover the bottom. When it is hot, put the patties in (you will probably need to do this in two lots, adding new oil to the second batch). Fry for two minutes on the first side, then turn and cook for three minutes longer. Drain on kitchen paper and eat with halves of lemon for squeezing and a watercress or frisée salad.

Enough for 3

125g/5 handfuls of fresh white
    breadcrumbs
400g crabmeat
half a teaspoon of cayenne pepper
3 tablespoons grain mustard
a tablespoon of Worcestershire
    sauce
3 spring onions, chopped
4 heaped tablespoons mayonnaise
a handful/5 tablespoons chopped
    parsley
juice of half a lemon
oil

Mussels

The original ten-minute supper. A pot of blue-black mussels steams in seconds with a glass of wine and a handful of aromatics – by which I mean parsley, peppercorns and a bay leaf. The bay will do nothing in terms of flavour, but it does look the part. You can be too practical. Covered with a tight lid and cooked till the shells open, three minutes or less, there will be supper in no time at all. And the steam, fishy and salty, will smell wonderful. Pull the little wobbly orange mussels apart with your fingers and dunk your bread in the broth.

Once in a while I gild the lily, the clear fishy essence of the *moules marinière*, with a dash of cream (you can't really beat it, so why get fancy?).

Mussels with tarragon and cream

Serves 2
500g cleaned mussels
a shallot, finely chopped
2 garlic cloves, crushed
butter, a thick slice
a handful of tarragon sprigs
a few sprigs of thyme
Pernod
50ml (2 or 3 tablespoons) cream

Give the mussels the once over. They should be free of grit and sand and there should be no broken shells. Discard any that do not shut when you tap them firmly on the edge of the sink. Cook the shallot and garlic in half of the butter in a deep pan, one to which you can find a lid. When the shallot is soft but barely coloured, tear the leaves off the tarragon and add most of them to the onion. Chuck in the thyme, too. Add the mussels and cover tightly with a lid.

Let the mussels steam, shaking the pot from time to time, for three minutes until they are open. There may be a few that refuse to budge; throw them away. Scoop out the mussels with a slotted slice or spoon into a warm bowl. Tip the cooking liquor through a fine sieve into a bowl. Rinse out the pan (be quick, the mussels are getting cold), then return the pan to the heat. Pour in the strained cooking liquor, a few glugs of Pernod, a couple of tablespoons will do, then pour in the cream and throw in the rest of the tarragon leaves. Let the sauce bubble for a minute or so, then tip it over the mussels. Fab.

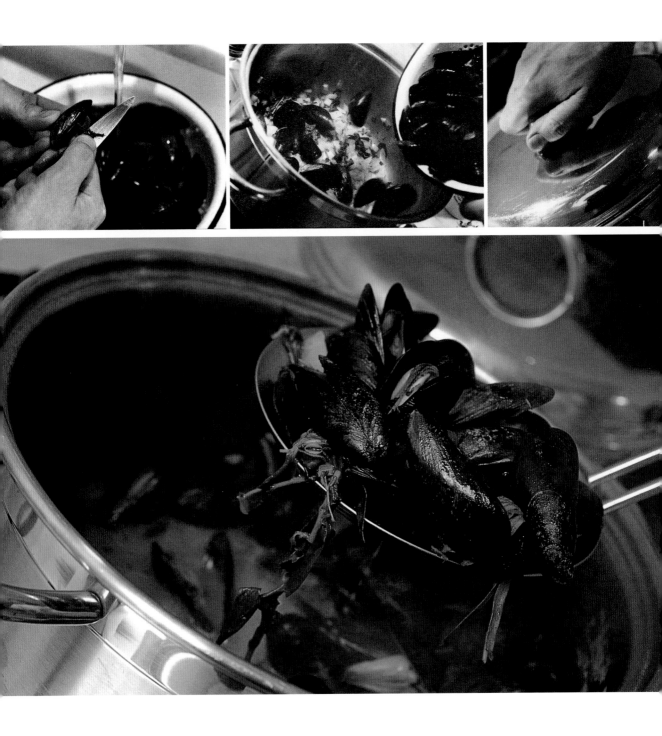

Chicken
& Other Birds

A chicken – its shining skin crisp, its flesh soft and buttery – is a splendid thing to bring to the table. Especially if the cook hasn't mucked about with it. Only a fool would cook a chicken devoid of its golden skin, basted with oil or butter or both. Roasted, grilled or cooked in shallow butter, the skin crisps, bulging and glistening in the heat. Seasoned with a little too much salt and a squeeze of lemon or a spoonful of the cooking juices, the skin of the chicken is almost as good to eat as its flesh. Sod the skin-less chicken breast imprisoned on its blue polystyrene tray. Chicken for those who don't really like chicken.

A free range bird of an old-fashioned breed, big and fat (and jolly dear), roasted till its flesh melts from its bones, is a dinner that appeals to almost everyone. Not fancy cooking, but fine ingredients treated simply. When I hear cries of boredom at such plain, unfussy cooking, I know that the chicken was not of the best. How dare anyone tire of such glorious, sumptuous eating. It is a grand palate indeed that sneers at a fine roast bird.

A chicken will thank us for a restrained gilding of butter, garlic and herbs. A few spices perhaps, or a slosh of white wine. It will hate us if we treat it like a lump of tofu – as neat protein to soak up stronger flavours like a sponge. A plain roast or grilled chicken is cause enough for celebration. Go for a big bird – it will not be tough. You will have enough for the whole family, plus a stout carcass for stock and rich pickings for those who do not mind working for their supper. Cold chicken sandwiches, with salt and mayo, are a treat indeed.

Ignore those who tempt us to bone and stuff, sauce and garnish. The best meal in the world is one that includes a huge roast bird served warm rather than hot, with some soft lettuce as a leafy sop for its juices, and a big dish of roast potatoes. A whole small cheese on the table, a Cheddar perhaps or something from the Dales, and you truly have a meal to celebrate.

There is more. Quail, pheasant and duck offer good pickings too. Their flesh is richer, their flavour gamey and dark. They must not be overcooked. Or overlooked. These are birds that are at the supermarket, perhaps the butchers too, and have toothsome, sweet flesh and good bones for us to chew. They are not as fancy as they sound, and provide good eating. If we can tear ourselves away from the sumptuous flesh of the chicken.

Roast chicken

For 4

a plump free-range chicken, about
   2kg

75g butter

3 large cloves of garlic

a few bay leaves

a branch of thyme

4 large potatoes, peeled

lemon juice

A plainly roasted bird, seasoned only with butter, garlic and the most basic aromatics like bay and thyme, its flavour unsmothered by stuffing, bread sauce and the like. Its juices are served as they are, devoid of the flour and stock of traditional thick gravy. The point of cooking the bird with potatoes is to soak up some of the buttery juices from the chicken, rendering them crisp and gooey outside, melting within. A few leaves of soft, old fashioned lettuce to soak up the juices on the plate seems to me more appropriate than the usual carrots and sprouts.

Set the oven at 230°C/450°F/Gas 8. Pull out the bag of giblets, if there is one, from inside the bird, then rinse it inside and out, patting the skin dry with kitchen paper. A wet chicken will not crisp. Smear the butter over the bird, being particularly generous around the breast, where the flesh is inclined to dryness. Season unsparingly with salt and pepper. Stuff the unpeeled garlic cloves wherever they will fit. Tuck in the bay and thyme.

Cut the potatoes into large hunks. Too small and they will be all crisp skin and no soft centre. Put them around the bird in the bottom of the tin. Roast the chicken and potatoes for fifteen minutes. The skin will tighten. It may even colour here and there. Turn the heat down to 190°C/375°F/Gas 5. Spoon the melted butter in the pan over the bird. Roast for forty-five minutes.

Baste the bird with the juices that are collecting in the pan. Do this a couple of times during roasting and turn the potatoes at the same time so that all their sides turn crisp and gold.

The chicken is done when its juices run clear, without any pinkness. Tip the bird gently in its tin to gauge this, or pierce a fat thigh with a skewer. The legs should give slightly when pulled. The skin should be blistered, golden and brown. The ends of its legs should be a little charred. It should smell wonderful.

Remove the bird from the oven and lift carefully, for it is hot and slippery, on to a warm serving plate. Leave it to rest for ten minutes before carving, it will stay moister that way. Carve it directly from the oven and you can watch its precious juices escaping. Turn the oven up to the original temperature. Put the potatoes back. The juices will bubble and spit, the potatoes will crisp and a brown stickiness will adhere to them (actually the caramelising of the cooking juices).

Remove them when they are golden, crisp and gooey but before the juices burn.

Carve the chicken on to warm plates. Serve a handful of potatoes on to each plate and spoon over the cooking juices from the pan, seasoned with a little more salt and lifted with a squeeze or two of lemon juice.

Herbed roast chicken

It is mostly robust, shrubby herbs that add interest to a roast bird –
woody thyme and rosemary rather than leafy basil and coriander.
Fragile tarragon defies the rule. Sage works but can be coarse in quantity. Scatter loose leaves or sprigs over the skin and stuff a stem or two
inside the rib cage, where its aroma might filter through to the flesh.
Add them once the chicken has had its first blast in the hot oven. Any

earlier and they will burn to a crisp before they have given their flavour away to the bird.

I grow several thymes and have used them all with roast chicken. Lemon thyme is charming, the rest no different from common or garden *Thymus officinalis*. The sort you get from the supermarket. My other favourite roast chicken herbs are tarragon, whose aniseed notes go particularly well, and bay. Tuck bay leaves round the bird. Sometimes I scatter a small handful of dried *herbes de Provence* over instead. Especially if it is too wet and slippery to negotiate the herb patch. The melange of thyme, bay, basil, lavender and savory is more fragrant than one expects of a dried herb mix.

If I am adding herbs, I also add lemon. Not to the finished juices this time but to the bird itself. Squeeze the juice of a lemon, or even two if they are small, over the chicken after buttering. Stuff the lemon shells inside the bird. Together, the addition of herbs and lemon produces a result more fragrant, more aromatic and altogether more tempting than our traditional bullying sage and onion stuffing.

The best bits

Good housekeeping is often at odds with good eating. An overzealous hand with the clearing up, springing up from the table and throwing too much, too soon into the sink, can destroy in seconds what is so important to the intelligent cook. The glorious dripping and jelly that will enrich a sauce, the gelatinous bones, sucked or not, that will make a glowing, golden broth, not to mention the crunchy, sticky bits of skin and potato stuck to the pan that are such a treat for the greedy.

While the carcass is still warm it makes sense to strip the meat from the bones. This takes little more than ten minutes. Tear away the flesh and skin, including any juicy buttons of meat hiding underneath, but not so thoroughly as to render the bones uninteresting enough for soup, then put the meat somewhere cool to await reincarnation as a sandwich or risotto. All the meat is worth eating, but because of its various shapes and textures it is best used in different ways.

Second helpings of roast chicken

If you are blessed with neat slices and juicy lumps of brown meat from the legs then I suggest you eat them with little more than pickled walnuts, gherkins or red cabbage, and some hot boiled waxy potatoes. A wobbling, shining lump of home-made mayonnaise, deep greeny-yellow with olive oil and thick enough to cut with a knife, would be my only other accompaniment. That, and very crisp, fresh bread. Oh, and plenty of coarse sea salt to crumble over the meat.

... and the rest

There will be less attractive (at least to look at) pieces of chicken, too. There will be stringy bits, dry bits and juicy bits. All will have flavour. All are too interesting to waste. With luck there will also be the little nuggets of flesh from under the carcass – in particular the two small oysters of flesh that lie where the legs join the backbone. There will be jelly. There will be unidentifiable, savoury, crusty bits. All of which will make an interesting sauce for wide, slithery noodles if you warm them gently in a heavy-based pan with enough cream almost to cover them, a handful of chopped fresh tarragon and plenty of salt and finely ground pepper. Or you could bake the same with breadcrumbs to give a crisp coat.

With cream and mustard

Tear the chicken into bite-sized pieces. Toss them in a bowl with the cream, cheese, a loose handful of tarragon leaves, mustard and a little salt. Don't forget to add any jelly and tasty bits rescued from the underside of the carcass. Tip into a shallow ovenproof dish, cover with a layer of breadcrumbs and bake till the crumbs are crisp and the outer edge is bubbling (200°C/400°F/Gas 6 for 20 minutes).

For 2 as a light meal with salad

2 large handfuls of cooked chicken

a breakfast cup/about 300ml pot of double cream

a handful of grated cheese (anything will do)

a little tarragon

a heaped tablespoon of grain mustard

2 handfuls of fresh breadcrumbs

With smoked bacon, shallots and toast

Melt the dripping in a shallow pan over a moderate heat. Fry the shallots and garlic in the dripping until they soften and turn golden at the edges. Add the bacon and continue cooking while the bacon fat turns golden and translucent. At this point you should start the toast.

Stir in the chicken pieces, including any jelly and bits of skin that look as if they may turn crisp and interesting, and season with a little chopped thyme if you have it. No salt. Pour in the wine and turn up the heat. Let it bubble and steam until only a little liquid is left, at which point grind over a little black pepper and lift the chicken and shallots out on to the buttered toast with a draining spoon, leaving behind the liquid.

Add the butter, which should be cold from the fridge rather than oily from the kitchen, and whisk until the juices and butter become a thin sauce – only a matter of a minute or two. Make sure to scrape up the crusty golden deposits stuck to the pan – there's a lot of flavour there. Let it bubble once or twice, taste it for seasoning, then pour it over the toast. Eat immediately.

For 1 as a light meal

2 tablespoons dripping

2 shallots, finely sliced

a clove of garlic, crushed

a large handful of diced smoked bacon or lardons

2 handfuls of cooked chicken

a little thyme, if you have it

a wineglass of red wine

a large knob of chilled butter, about the size of a walnut in its shell

2 rounds of hot, buttered toast

Golden skin and savoury juices

A chicken is undemanding of the cook. Smeared with butter, seasoned with salt, thyme and pepper and thrown in a hot oven for around an hour, the bird will emerge a golden, tender feast. It will even have made gravy for us with the butter and its own cooking juices.

Yet I could cry for the chicken. Our greed has downgraded such a feast into a bundle of flabby white flesh and brittle bones – a shadow of the crisp-skinned, juicy-fleshed and succulent bird it once was. As soon as our ferocious demand for cheap protein took the proud, almost self-sufficient bird out of the farmyard and into crowded, cheek-by-jowl indoor accommodation, the chicken ceased to be a treat.

Encouragingly, farmers who keep old-fashioned, big-boned breeds and let them scavenge in grass or woodland for at least some of their food, providing corn and shelter should they want it, are increasing in number. Cut our consumption of chicken to one free range bird a fortnight instead of intensively farmed, cling-wrapped joints twice a week, and we could slowly introduce in our young cooks a little respect for the tender, savoury flesh of the chicken. And perhaps restore it in our older ones.

A bird that has had a (true) free range existence will

recompense the extra we have had to pay for it by giving us rich, golden broth from its bones. Intensively farmed birds make poor stock – their weak bones offer no goodness to the cook. The outdoor bird will have richer, darker flesh, more gamey and interesting, and the bones more tasty to chew. I wonder whether a farm labourer would make better eating than a bank clerk.

Versatile and value for money, a chicken can provide a celebratory roast and a warming broth for the next day. Stripped from the bones, the spare flesh can be transformed into a creamy pie, topped with crumbs or pastry, or a rich sauce for noodles. Cut into portions, the bird could instead be fried with herbs and cream or stewed with spices and yoghurt. Bones removed, it could be grilled till sweet and lightly charred and eaten with salt and a garlic-scented butter.

Roast chicken broth

For 4

2 heaped tablespoons dripping

2 medium-sized onions, roughly chopped

2 sticks celery, sliced in small chunks

a small lump of ginger, about the size of a walnut

4 medium-sized dark brown mushrooms (if they are a little old and sweaty, then all to the good)

the chicken carcass and any spare bones

brandy – a double measure

2 wineglasses of red wine

bay leaves, sprigs of thyme, celery leaves, parsley sprigs

2 handfuls of orzo (rice-shaped pasta) or small brown lentils

a small handful of chopped parsley

Only the wasteful will fail to make a broth of the bones. Quantities here can be imprecise, timing inaccurate. What is important is not to allow the liquid to do anything more energetic than shudder and 'glup'. An enthusiastic boil will muddy both colour and flavour.

Melt the dripping in a deep, heavy pan. When it bubbles add the onions and celery. Cook until the vegetables start to brown, stirring once or twice. Add the ginger, cut into thin slices, and the mushrooms, halved or quartered. Cook for a minute or two till the mushrooms have softened, then add the carcass and bones. Don't forget the giblets and all the bits of jelly hiding under the chicken bones. You can forget the string. Cook until the chicken is brown – though it will only be so in patches. The less you move it around the quicker that will be.

Pour in the brandy and wine and allow to boil furiously, which will evaporate the alcohol, leaving only its flavour behind. While there is still liquid in the pot add enough water almost to cover the carcass. You will need about a litre. Throw in a few herbs, fresh or dried, such as thyme, bay, the leaves from the celery or a few fennel sprigs, and about half a dozen black peppercorns, lightly cracked. And a little salt.

Bring slowly towards boiling point, but turn the heat down before it actually gets there (with a large spoon, skim the frothy scum that appears and discard). The liquid should just shudder, sending up a few bubbles now and again and emitting a regular 'glup'. Boil it and you will spoil it. Let the broth cook gently for just over an hour.

Pour the broth through a colander set over another pan. Discard the jumble of vegetables and bones after they have dripped a while, then return the broth to the original saucepan – it will still have a little flavoursome sludge stuck to the bottom. Bring back to the boil, add the pasta or lentils (or pearl barley or whole wheat if that is what you have) and simmer for fifteen to twenty minutes till tender. Taste and add more salt, ground black or white pepper or perhaps a little sherry. Stir in the chopped parsley. Serve very hot, in big comforting bowls with a couple of slices from a nice fresh loaf.

A simple sauté

The joy of the sauté is the crusty, savoury sediment that builds up under the meat while it cooks, and which becomes the base for a simple sauce. No commercial cube or powder can replicate the sticky, golden-brown deposit left behind after a joint of chicken has been cooked in butter. No elaborate, separately made sauce can beat an integral one made from the pan juices of the meat it is to accompany.

Chicken for sautéing, in other words for frying quickly in shallow fat, needs plenty of skin to crisp in the heat and a bone inside to ensure succulent eating. Boned and skinned chicken breasts from a supermarket tray will give a dry and pointless result. Thighs, with their juicy brown meat, generous skin and thick bones have much to offer. Drumsticks and breasts are suitable but can err to dryness at the thin end.

So thighs it is. Butter will enrich them, olive oil will stop them burning. The sauce will be nothing more than the caramelised juices from the pan, a little white wine, a herb and some cream.

With tarragon and cream

Melt the butter in a shallow, solid pan over a moderate heat. Add the oil and when the fat starts to froth add the chicken, skin-side down. It will spit at you from time to time. Cook until the skin is pale gold, then turn the meat and add half the tarragon. Turn the heat down a little. Continue cooking, the pan covered by a lid, the butter sizzling but not furiously so, until the chicken is a golden reddish brown. A matter of ten to fifteen minutes. Avoid moving the chicken too much as this will result in a lack of the sticky deposits you need to make the sauce.

Pierce the thickest part of the thigh with a skewer, or one of the prongs of the fork you turned it with. If the juices run clear then it is cooked. If there are specks of blood then it will need a little longer. Remove the chicken to a warm plate, pouring most of the fat off (holding the tarragon back with a draining spoon) and storing for later use.

Turn up the heat. Return the pan to the heat and pour in the wine. Let it bubble, then, using a wooden spoon, scrape at the crusty brown deposits – the caramelised juices – left by the chicken. They will dissolve into the wine. Toss in the rest of the tarragon. Pour in the cream, stirring it into the wine. Return the chicken, and the juices that have run from it, to the pan. Let the sauce bubble until it has reduced by half, watching it closely. It will disappear if you turn your back. Taste the sauce and add salt if you like. As the sauce bubbles for a minute or two, stir in a squeeze of lemon juice to stop it from cloying. Accompany with green beans and bread to mop the plate.

For 2 as a main dish

a large knob of butter, about the size of a walnut in its shell

a tablespoon of olive oil

4 large chicken thighs

a generous palmful of tarragon leaves (about 30 large leaves, 40 small)

a small glass of white wine

100ml double cream or 3 heaped tablespoons crème fraîche

a squeeze of lemon juice

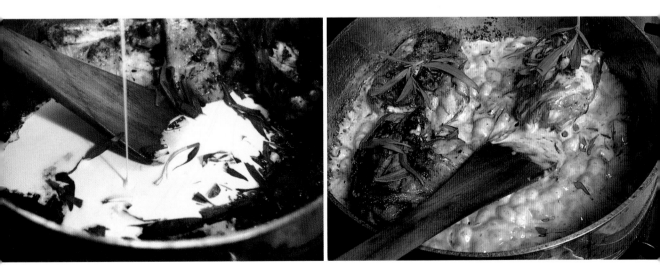

A fragrant sauté with butter and cardamom

For 2, as a main dish with rice

8 green cardamom pods

a rounded teaspoon of coriander
seeds

2 large knobs of butter – a good
50g and possibly more

4 chicken thighs

2 medium-sized onions, roughly
chopped

3 garlic cloves, crushed to a pulp

half a teaspoon of ground
turmeric

200ml mixed thick yoghurt and
double cream

a handful of coriander leaves

Crush the cardamom pods with a pestle or heavy weight, discard the green papery husks and grind the fifty or so little brown seeds to a powder in a mortar or coffee grinder. Gently heat the whole coriander seeds in a dry frying pan for a couple of minutes. Once they are golden brown and fragrant, grind them too.

Melt the butter in a heavy low-sided casserole or sauté pan. Fry the chicken in this, skin-side down and slowly so that the butter does not burn, until the skin is golden. Turn and continue cooking. When the outside is pale golden lift the chicken out with a draining spoon. Add the onions and the garlic, together with a little more butter if there is not much left in the pan. Cook slowly until the onions are translucent and soft, about ten to fifteen minutes.

Stir the ground coriander and cardamom into the onions. Add the turmeric, which will give depth and colour to the dish, and cook for two minutes, stirring so that it does not burn. Return the chicken to the pan. Pour in enough boiling water to come half-way up the chicken, and about half a teaspoonful of sea salt. Cover and, stirring occasionally, simmer for twenty-five minutes (the liquid should bubble quietly under the lid), by which time the chicken should be tender, but far from falling off the bones, and the crusty deposits from the pan will have dissolved into the sauce.

Stir in the yoghurt and cream and grind over a little black pepper. Bring slowly to the boil but do not actually let it do so, then stir quickly with a small whisk, although it will curdle to some extent. Taste and perhaps add more salt or pepper. Scatter over the coriander leaves, torn a little to release their fragrance, and replace the lid, removing it at the table when plates are passed.

Sticky chicken wings with lemon

Hot, savoury bones to gnaw at. Sticky, juicy fingers to lick.

Pull any remaining feathers from the wing tips. Dust lightly with flour. Heat the olive oil in a shallow pan over a moderate heat. When the oil crackles and shimmers, add the chicken wings. They will spit at you if the oil is hot enough. Cook, without moving them, until they are golden on one side, a good five minutes, then turn them over. Season with salt. Cover with a lid and leave to cook, the heat turned a little lower, until the wings are golden and sticky. About thirty minutes, maybe a little longer, it will hardly matter.

Season with salt. Be generous. Lift the wings out, leaving behind any golden-brown goo that has stuck to the pan. Turn up the heat. Pour in the lemon juice and put the butter in the pan. Shake the pan, scraping at any crusty deposits (that's where the flavour is) with a spatula. About five minutes later the pan juices, gooey bits, butter and lemon will have combined to form an impromptu sauce. Pour over the chicken wings and eat while hot, with your fingers.

For 2

a handful of chicken wings per person (probably about 4 free range, or 6–8 economy jobbies)
a little flour
olive oil (about 4 tablespoons)
juice of 2 large lemons
a lump of butter, about 50g

Roast chicken thighs with lime juice and ginger

Put the chicken pieces in a stainless steel roasting tin, then cut slashes across their skin, cutting slightly down into the flesh. Mix the lime juice, sliced lemon grass, chopped chillies, shredded ginger, spring onions, garlic and honey together. Stir in a good teaspoon of salt. Pour the resulting slush over the chicken pieces, rubbing it well into the slits. Set aside for a good hour or two, turning the chicken once in its marinade.

Heat the oven to 200°C/400°F/Gas 6. Place the roasting tin in the oven and cook until the chicken is golden and fragrant, about forty to forty-five minutes.

For 2

6 chicken thighs
juice of 4 limes
2 stalks of lemon grass, thinly sliced
4 small, hot red chillies, seeded and chopped
a large lump of ginger, about the size of a walnut, shredded
4 spring onions, chopped
2 large cloves of garlic, chopped
3 tablespoons honey

Grilled chicken

The best grilled chicken is that cooked over the ash-covered coals and herbs of an outdoor barbecue, where the woodsmoke penetrates the meat and the fresh air has sharpened the appetite. But it is the most unpredictable method of cooking. We have less control over the heat of a barbecue than an oven or hob, yet squandering such delights on the annual display of garden pyrotechnics is a waste. A cook must occasionally compromise.

We can grill a piece of chicken to perfection on a ridged cast iron griddle. The sort I talk about in the chapter headed Pots, Pans & Heat. By perfection I mean hot, crisp-skinned and juicy within. It should have a skin that is amber in parts, almost black in others, the underside should be sticky, its juices sweet from the heat, and it should taste deeply savoury in the mouth. Preferably a little too hot, too, so that it has to dance around our mouth while we make pointless blowing and sucking noises. And it must have some good sea salt on it, probably more than is good for us.

We cannot hope to achieve a similar result with an overhead domestic grill. Though it will make a good round of toast if you get it hot enough. Meat needs to touch the bars of the grill, whether it be over the glowing ashes of a barbecue (a pretty hit-and-miss affair in my experience) or pressed down on to the ridges and furrows of a cast iron grill pan. The skin is most savoury where it has touched the bars.

The smoke is the thing. Copious amounts fill my kitchen, and

therefore my living room when the oiled chicken hits the red-hot iron. But it is worth the discomfort to have the herby smoke flavour the meat. You cannot do that with an overhead grill. It is partly the smoke that gives appeal to the campfire chicken. That and the feel of the slightly charred meat between our teeth and hot, salty juices dribbling down our chins.

A creamy, piquant sauce for grilled chicken

A luscious, slightly tart and almost instant sauce for a piece of grilled chicken – be it a boned leg, a breast or a thigh – cooked on a griddle placed over the hob as in the following recipes, over the flames of a barbecue or even under an overhead grill.

Enough for 2
250g crème fraîche
grainy French mustard
bottled green peppercorns
a handful of chopped parsley

Tip the crème fraîche into a small saucepan and place over a gentle heat. As it starts to thin, slowly stir in a seasoning of mustard, green peppercorns, salt and black pepper. I suggest you start with a couple of tablespoons of mustard, two teaspoons of green peppercorns and then see how you feel about it. Stick your finger in and taste it, you might want to add more of either or both or even a few drops of the lip-smacking liquid from the peppercorn bottle. Stir in the parsley. Turn the heat up a little so that the sauce bubbles enthusiastically, all the time reducing in quantity and thickening in consistency. After three or four minutes you should have a tantalising, sharp and creamy sauce, the consistency of thick pouring cream to eat with your grilled chicken.

Put the chicken pieces on warm plates and spoon over the sauce.

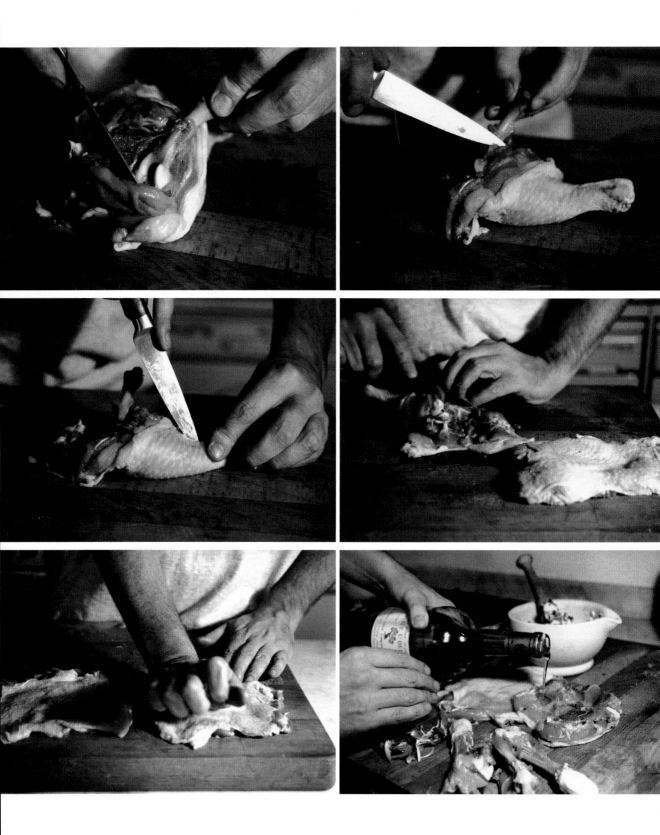

Grilled chicken with butter and balsamic vinegar

Grilled chicken with mellow, piquant, buttery juices. Salad leaves of some sort would be a good accompaniment, as would a pile of the grilled or fried onions on page 134. Fat thighs, free range from a good butcher, are a much tastier option than the silly little things stocked by most of the supermarkets.

Smear both sides of the chicken with olive oil. Be generous. Season with a little salt. But not much. Get a griddle pan hot on the hob. You can use an overhead grill instead but the results will not be nearly as pleasing. Slap the meat on the grill, pressing it down hard with a palette knife. There will be much smoke and spitting. Don't move it for at least two minutes, then turn it over, lower the heat slightly and cook for a further seven or eight minutes. Pour a little balsamic vinegar over the chicken; a tablespoon between the two should be enough. Squeeze over some lemon juice, slide two lumps of butter, each about the size of a walnut, on to the chicken, add salt, grind over some pepper, then eat while all is hot, buttery and sizzling.

» Removing the bone from a chicken thigh is a doddle. Just put the thigh skin-side down on a chopping board and find the bone. With a sharp, small knife, cut along either side of the bone. Hold the bone with the fingertips of one hand, cutting it away from the meat with the other. Flatten the meat a little with your fist or a rolling pin. But don't bash it to shreds.

For 2

2 large chicken thighs, boned and flattened, or breasts if you must
olive oil
balsamic vinegar
half a lemon
butter

Grilled chicken with thyme leaves, salt and garlic butter

For 2

2 boned chicken legs (or breasts
    if you must)
olive oil
a tablespoon of thyme leaves
a couple of plump, new cloves of
    juicy garlic
about 50g soft butter
a small handful of chopped
    parsley
a lemon
sea salt flakes – not crystals

My insistence that brown meat is more succulent than white is nowhere better illustrated than on the grill. But provided a boned breast has its skin attached it should grill to a tasty enough result, especially if it is left whole. My first choice is the legs from a fat, free-range bird that have had their bones removed to give two near rectangles of flesh. Ask your butcher (though point out he should not skin them too) or have a go yourself with one eye on the photographs on page 82. It will take you all of fifteen minutes.

Get the griddle pan hot. This means leaving it for three or four minutes over the gas burner or electric ring till you can feel the heat rising from the pan. Meanwhile, rub both flesh and skin side of the chicken with a generous amount of olive oil and the thyme leaves. You can use groundnut oil but not walnut (which burns too easily) or extra virgin olive (which would be a waste).

Slap each piece of chicken on the hot grill skin-side down. If the grill is hot enough it will crackle and spit. Leave the meat in place for a full two minutes. The skin will turn a healthy colour. The flesh will tighten and shrink. Press the meat down on the grill with a palette knife or similar – (splutter, pop, bang). Turn the meat over and cook for a further seven or eight minutes, till cooked through and golden brown on each side. The flesh should be juicy.

Meanwhile, peel and crush the garlic and mix it with the parsley, butter and the juice of the lemon. A pestle and mortar is good for this. It will take all of two minutes. When the chicken is cooked, crumble over the sea salt and serve with a dollop of the lemon garlic butter.

A creamy, colourful, fragrant chicken curry

For 2

For the marinade:

10 green cardamom pods

a teaspoon of cumin seeds

half a teaspoon of dried chilli
flakes

vegetable or groundnut oil

4 large, plump chicken thighs

For the sauce:

vegetable or groundnut oil

2 medium-sized onions, roughly
chopped

a knob of ginger, about as big as
your thumb

3 plump, juicy cloves of garlic,
thinly sliced

a bunch of coriander leaves and
stalks

a teaspoon of dried chilli flakes

a teaspoon of cumin seeds

half a teaspoon of ground
turmeric

6 tomatoes, chopped

4 heaped tablespoons natural
yoghurt

juice of half a small lemon

4 heaped tablespoons crème
fraîche

A seriously unauthentic dish this, but who gives a monkey's for authenticity? All that really matters is whether something is good to eat. And this is. It is neither Thai nor Indian. A few purists are going to be really pissed-off, especially about the crème fraîche. Don't be put off by the length of the recipe – it is truly a doddle. Do it one weekend.

Break the cardamom pods open and pick out the little black seeds. Put them in a pestle and mortar with the cumin seeds and crush them coarsely. Alternatively just put them in a plastic bag and crush them with a rolling pin. Tip them into a shallow dish with the chilli flakes, a teaspoon of salt and a few grinds of black pepper. Pour over enough oil to make a thin paste (about 2 tablespoons) then rub it all over the chicken. Don't you dare take the chicken skin off. It will be part of the joy of the dish when it's all crisp and golden. Set aside for thirty minutes.

Pour enough oil into a deep, heavy pan just to cover the bottom. It will be a couple of tablespoons or so. Place over a moderate heat and add the chopped onions, the ginger – peeled and thinly sliced – and the garlic. Stir from time to time, cooking until the onions are transparent – about ten minutes. Add half the coriander and its stalks, roughly chopped, the chilli, cumin and turmeric. Cook for a further two minutes then remove from the pan.

Pour in a little more oil, turn the heat up a bit, and put in the marinated chicken, skin side down. Leave until the skin has coloured a little, then turn and cook the other side. Watch carefully so that the chicken does not burn. It should turn golden without browning. If there is much oil then pour some of it away. Return the onions to the pan, add the chopped tomatoes and the yoghurt. Stir, making sure that some of the mixture goes under the chicken. Let the mixture come to the boil. The colours will be vivid. The smells will be great. It will be yellow, green and red. Like a Howard Hodgkin. Cover with a lid and leave to simmer gently for thirty minutes. An occasional stir will help. Get the oven hot.

Remove the chicken pieces and place them on an ovenproof dish. Sprinkle them with salt and place in a preheated oven at 220°C/425°F/Gas 8. Turn up the heat under the sauce, squeeze in the lemon juice, and let it bubble excitedly. Stir it from time to time.

You can scoop off some of the orange oil that comes to the surface, but there is no need to be too pernickety. When all has reduced to a thick slush, a matter of four or five minutes, stir in the crème fraîche and the rest of the coriander. Season it with salt and black pepper. Remove the chicken, which with luck will have gone slightly crispy, and put two pieces of chicken on each plate and spoon over some of the sauce. Eat with soft, warm Indian breads or, of course, rice.

Hot and sour grilled chicken soup

A clear, bright-tasting soup. A quick one, too.

Brush the chicken strips with oil and grill them till golden brown. Try not to overcook them. Transfer them to a medium-sized saucepan and pour over the stock, then bring to the boil and add the garlic, chillies, lemon grass, lime leaves and fish sauce. Simmer at a gentle pace for about ten minutes. Add the spring onions and the lime juice and simmer, with a little salt and ground black pepper added, for a further five minutes. Stir in the coriander leaves and serve steaming hot.

For 2

500g chicken breasts or thighs, cut into thin strips

a little groundnut oil

1.5 litres good, rich home-made or ready-made chicken stock (not from a cube this time)

2 cloves of garlic, finely chopped

2 small red chillies, seeded and chopped

2 stalks of lemon grass, peeled, chopped and crushed

6 lime leaves, rolled up tightly and finely shredded

a tablespoon of Thai fish sauce (nam pla)

4 spring onions, finely sliced

juice of a lime

a handful of coriander leaves, chopped

Hot Thai stir fry

For 2

a generous handful of basil
    leaves (at least 20)
groundnut oil
350g chicken, cut into small
    pieces but skin left on
4 spring onions, roughly chopped
small lump of ginger, about the
    size of a walnut, peeled and
    shredded
3 garlic cloves, thinly sliced
2 hot red chillies, seeded and
    finely chopped
2 tablespoons dark soy sauce

A quick, hot disguise for inferior supermarket chicken pieces. Made with decent chicken the dish will sing even louder. Some rice might be a good idea as this is not a substantial dish – more of a light supper.

Tear the basil leaves up a bit. Heat a wok or deep frying pan and then pour in enough oil to cover the bottom, probably about two table-spoons. When the oil starts to shimmer and smoke, drop in the chopped chicken. If it lands skin-side down so much the better. Do not touch until the bottom side is golden, then move the chicken around in the pan. Chopsticks are as good as anything for this and will seem appropriate, though any old spoon is fine. Cook until the meat is golden on all sides. Test a piece; it should be juicy and only just cooked through. Tip out into a dish (anything will do, it is going back in the pan later).

Add a little more oil to the pan if there seems little left. Throw in the spring onions, ginger and garlic. Shake it all about a bit. It should sizzle and spit. If it doesn't then your pan isn't hot enough. Add the chillies. When they soften, return the chicken to the pan, throw in the basil and stir for a minute. Slosh in the soy sauce and serve on hot plates.

Duck

A duck tempts us with its promise of crisp skin and rich meat – especially when that rich meat is spiced in the Eastern manner with aniseed, clove and orange. The English way, the bird roasted plain with apple sauce and stuffing, is, I think, often underrated. As is the Sixties restaurant cliché of duck with orange sauce – a dashing dish when properly made.

Ignore those who argue that duck is all fat and no meat – they are missing the point. The fat makes the otherwise dry meat succulent (any excess is removed before cooking). Just allow a medium-sized duck for two. What is essential, to my mind, is that a duck is cooked with its bones. Compare the flavour of a whole roast duck with one of those boneless breasts (or *magret*) the French have such a taste for. The whole roast bird is a wonderful tangle of bones, sticky fat and crisp skin. The celebrated *magret* is nothing more than a big lump of protein. And not a very interesting one at that. What is more, picking the hot, sweet meat from a duck carcass can be a joy.

Cumin, coriander seed (with its orange overtones) and aniseed all flatter the meat of the duck. So do the sweeter citrus fruits, salty green olives and tart apples. A cream sauce with duck is a misguided adventure, but fruit jellies such as redcurrant can be stirred into the gravy to great effect, provided they are not too sweet. The splendid dish of crispy duck with hoisin sauce and soft, dry pancakes is, I think, best left to the magic hands of Chinese restaurant chefs.

Roast duck with aniseed and bitter orange marmalade

For 2

a small- to medium-sized duck, about 2kg

4 large handfuls of fresh breadcrumbs (for which you will need a lump of bread about 15 x 10cm)

ginger, a piece roughly as big as your thumb

a tablespoon of five-spice powder

an apple

2 eggs, lightly beaten

6 heaped tablespoons orange marmalade

about half a dozen star anise

3 clementines

Star anise, the hard, beautiful, star-shaped spice, is to be found in oriental grocers' shops and major supermarkets. You will also need some salad leaves to soak up the juices left on your plate. Try chicory. Don't be put off by the length of this recipe – it is dead easy.

If the duck has got its bits and pieces tucked inside in a plastic bag, then pull them out. Pull out any lumps of fat. Put the kettle on and put the duck in the sink. When the kettle boils, pour the boiling water over the duck. The skin will tighten and the excess fat will dissolve and run out. Pat the bird dry with kitchen paper.

Set the oven at 200°C/400°F/Gas 6. Put the breadcrumbs in a mixing bowl. Peel the ginger with a small knife and grate it into the bowl, then add the five-spice powder along with the apple. Don't bother to peel the apple. Season generously with both salt and ground black pepper. Stir in the lightly beaten eggs, half the marmalade and mix thoroughly.

Stuff the breadcrumb mixture inside the duck. It does not matter whether you use a spoon or your hands, or from which end you stuff it, though you will find it goes in the rear end more easily, despite the well-known saying. There is no need to fiddle around sewing it up, the stuffing is unlikely to fall out. And if it does it will simply roast in the pan instead.

Season the outside of the duck with salt, just a little, and place the duck in a roasting tin with the star anise. Pop it in the oven. After thirty minutes or so, take it out and pour off the fat that has collected in the roasting tin (put it in a cup in the fridge and fry potatoes in it later). Pour in about a teacup of water. Spread the rest of the marmalade over the duck. Cut the clementines in half and put them in the roasting tin. Put back in the oven.

After twenty minutes or so the clementines should be soft and juicy and the marmalade crusty in some places. Remove the tin from the oven and set aside for a minute or two. Lift the duck out on to a board or large plate and cut it in half. You will need a sharp, heavy knife for this. Simply cut down through the breast, the stuffing and the backbone. You need to put a bit of effort into it. Or, of course, you can carve it if you wish (probably best if your duck was on the large side. Just cut the legs off, slice off a few pieces of breast and let everyone pick away at the bones). Squash the clementines so that their juices leak into the pan juices, pour off any fat that comes to the top and bring to a rolling boil. Taste for seasoning (it might need a bit of pepper), then spoon over the duck and eat hot.

Pasta with lemon and thyme duck gravy

For 2

the duck carcass, giblets and
    wings
a handful (about 50g) chopped
    fatty bacon
2 fat cloves of garlic, squashed
    flat
a good pinch of dried chilli flakes
3 shallots or small onions, sliced
3 or 4 sprigs of thyme
grated zest of a small lemon
flour, a little
a wineglass/100ml red wine
    vinegar
500ml stock (if using a stock
    cube, then dilute with about
    twice as much water as the
    instructions suggest)
enough dried pasta for 2 (about
    300g)

A piquant, cold-weather sauce for pasta, made from the remains of the duck.

Smash the duck carcass about a bit, just so that the pieces are not too large. Fry the bacon in a deep saucepan till the fat is golden. Add the carcass, the giblets and wings and any jelly from the dish and cook over a high heat till it browns here and there. Throw in the garlic, chilli flakes, onions, thyme and lemon zest. Cook for ten minutes till all is golden brown and smells savoury, then add a couple of table-spoons of flour. Stir and continue to cook till the flour is golden. Pour in the vinegar. It will hiss and splutter a bit. Let it almost bubble away, then pour in the stock. Bring to the boil, then turn the heat down and simmer gently, partially covered with a lid, for thirty minutes.

    Cook the pasta in boiling, salted water. Pour the sauce from the bones and bits, squashing them against the side of the pan to extract all their goodness, then taste the sauce for salt and pepper. It will prob-ably need only the pepper, especially if you used a stock cube. Toss the cooked pasta in the hot duck sauce.

Potatoes cooked in the duck fat

For 2

450g potatoes, new, old, large,
    small – it matters not
4 heaped tablespoons duck fat
    saved from the roasting tin and
    cooled in the fridge
4 whole garlic cloves

Peel the potatoes if their skins are tough, otherwise don't bother. Cut them into large chunks (new potatoes in half), then toss them in a deep-sided shallow pan with the fat and the garlic cloves. Cover with a lid and let the potatoes cook over a medium to low heat until tender, about twenty-five minutes. Just before eating, pour off most of the fat, turn the heat up and season with salt. The potatoes will crisp lightly here and there, rendering them melting, golden and slightly crunchy at the same time.

Quail

Hot from the grill, rubbed with spices and mustard and its brittle bones cooked to a crisp, the quail is a small orgy of sweet flesh and spicy juices. Quail is finger food, and the finest feast of all for those who enjoy eating with their hands. A self-confessed connoisseur of finger licking, I rate a brace of grilled quail, hot and dripping with juice, as the most sensual eating there is. An orgy indeed.

But it is a tiny little thing, the quail. One per person seems mean, though two smacks of greed. Serve two. Forget the image of heather and tweeds, they are all farmed now, the strain coming from Japan rather than Scotland. Recipes for quail appear through Europe and the East, some are quite elaborate, but I have yet to find anything that beats a bird brushed with spiced butter and devoured straight from the grill.

Grilled mustard-butter quail

Get the grill hot – an overhead one is just as suitable here. Melt the butter in a small pan, then crush the garlic and stir into the butter with the mustard. Dip the birds into the butter, season with salt and black pepper and put them on their side on, or under, the grill. Cook for six minutes, then turn, drizzle with more mustard butter and cook the other side for about the same time. When all is sizzling and succulent, the skin perhaps singed slightly here and there, serve with a generous scattering of salt, a squeeze from the lemon and some crusty bread to mop up any stray juices. Only the narrow-minded would use a knife and fork.

For 2, as a light lunch
butter, about 75g
2 cloves of garlic
2 tablespoons Dijon mustard
4 oven-ready quail
lemon and French bread to serve

Pheasant

The earthy, gamey, autumnal flavours of the pheasant seem more appropriate to a special-occasion meal than to our daily cooking. The pheasant is weekend fare. Its price suggests as much. One bird will only feed two. That doesn't mean it shouldn't have a place in this book. Cooking is not just about throwing some pasta together for Wednesday supper before we dash out to a movie.

That said, I would do nothing fancy with a pheasant. Plainly roasted with a bit of bacon and a few potatoes is about as far as I would go. The bird's big flavours interfere with whatever we put with it, so a few flat, brown, velvet mushrooms thrown into the roasting tin near the end of cooking could serve as accompaniment, soaking up the cooking juices and saving us having to fart around with sprouts.

In the shops you may be offered a hen or a cock. A cock is bigger. Both are good eating. Just look for a bird that is plump and perky.

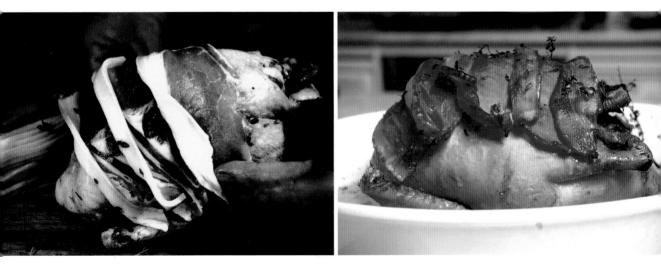

Roast pheasant with bacon, potatoes and white wine

A few roast potatoes, soft underneath from the roasting juices, and a bunch of watercress with which to scoop up the juices on the plate are, I think, more suitable here than a whole batch of more traditional vegetables, crumbs and sauces.

Put the bird in a roasting tin. Smear with the butter, dot with thyme sprigs, a few grinds of salt and black pepper, then wrap the rashers of bacon over the breasts and tuck the ends underneath. You need not make too much of this; we want them to curl up and be interesting.

Pour the wine into the tin, add the potatoes and place the bird in a hot oven (190°C/375°F/Gas 5) for thirty minutes. Remove the bacon from the bird (it will crisp in the tin), drop in the mushrooms, cut into four or six if they are large, and return the bird to the oven for a further fifteen to thirty minutes. A large cock will take about fifteen minutes more than a hen. The bird's juices will have soaked into the potatoes, but there may be a little impromptu gravy. The bird will be moist, you won't want much.

Remove from the oven and leave to settle for five or ten minutes. If you feel like carving the bird then do so, though you could cut the pheasant into four with a heavy knife or game scissors (I do not know anyone who actually owns such things, but they are very useful), then pour over any juices from the pan. Some crusty white bread and a few soft salad leaves, such as mâche, or better still watercress, would make an adequate accompaniment.

For 2 (unless it is a very large cock, which will feed 3)
a large pheasant (cock or hen, it matters not)
butter, two thick slices (about 50g)
a few sprigs of thyme
6 rashers of streaky bacon
a glass of white wine
2 medium-sized potatoes, each peeled and cut into about 6 chunks
4 medium-sized mushrooms

Pork, Bacon
& Sausages

From earliest times, a pig slaughtered in the autumn would keep a family going through the winter. First, a feast of fresh offal (faggots, perhaps, or kidneys sautéed with onion and sherry), then the rest salted or cured for winter storage. Trotters would be stuffed, ears crumbed and baked and extremities minced into sausages. But 'killing the pig' is beyond this cook, conjuring up as it does, a replay of Alan Bennett's *A Private Function*, with Maggie Smith chasing the squeaking, elusive, trotting Betty around the kitchen with the carving knife. It is still a meat for the cruel months.

Shop for pork, bacon and sausages at the butchers'; they seem to understand this meat more than the supermarkets who, in apparent response to their customers' requests, trim it of its fat and therefore its point. Although a pork steak, a slice of lean boneless meat from the loin, is a sound enough cut for a quick pan-fried supper (finish with cream and save the dish from cloying with a generous glop of mustard), it is the large joints for roasting that have most to commend them. Chops, especially if you can get the butcher to break EC regulations and sell them with the kidney, are worth buying if you intend to fry them in butter and oil and sharpen their pan juices with lemon. They will dry up on the grill.

The fattier cuts, such as strips of meat from the belly, take well to stir-frying in the Chinese manner. Their fat adds a voluptuous seasoning to vivid green pak choy leaves in the same way slices of smoked pork loin do to clean, sharp sauerkraut and boned pork shoulder does to the beans in a rustic cassoulet. While I do not despise the leaner cuts, I would no longer actively seek them out.

The classic pork dishes – roasted loin with fennel, sausage and mash, *porc aux pruneaux* and *char siu*, the red spiced Chinese roast – can only be improved by careful cooking, not by tinkering with and adding to. Its sticky fat demands a simple accompaniment of white chicory (braised in vegetable stock), green beans, boiled or roast potatoes and green salad. Pork is a meat for hearty, rustic cookery and seems uncomfortable in elegant surroundings. Rich meat for the cold and the hungry.

Pork casserole with mustard and lemon

The lardy meat of the pig's belly also makes the most unctuous of casseroles. A sticky stew for a cold night. Simmered slowly, barely bubbling in a moderately hot oven, the fat melts and lubricates the meat as it takes up the other seasonings. But it is a thin line between unctuous and cloying. Such a dish needs seasoning with something that has a bite to it – mustard or capers perhaps – and serving with a snappy salad such as crisp white cabbage dressed with lemon juice and peppery olive oil. From the cook it asks nothing more than patience and a stout appetite. This is not food for the fainthearted.

Cut the pork into large lumps, only slightly bigger than you would put in your mouth. Do not remove the fat, it is there to lubricate the meat. Peel and roughly chop the onions; size hardly matters when the cooking is long and slow. Peel and halve the garlic cloves. Cook the onions and garlic in the butter in a deep ovenproof pot, one to which you have a lid, over a moderate heat. After twenty minutes or so, with one or two stirrings, they will be soft and pale gold in colour. They will be mild and fragrant.

Remove the onions from the pan, leaving a few juices behind. Turn up the heat till the pan crackles and spits, then throw in the pork. Fry for three or four minutes till its fat has coloured, shaking it around occasionally, but not so often that it fails to colour.

Return the onions to the pan, grind over a little salt, about half a teaspoonful, then add a couple of bay leaves and a sprinkling of flour. Cover with a butter paper, then a tight lid, and put in a low oven at 150°C/300°F/Gas 2. Leave for one and a half hours. Remove the lid, stir in the capers, mustard, the juice of the lemon and its squeezed shells, cover again and continue cooking for twenty-five minutes.

Stir in the juices, then eat, scattered lightly with chopped parsley to brighten the flavour, and perhaps some plain boiled potatoes (nothing fancier) followed by some shredded crisp cabbage, chicory or frisée leaves to mop up the rich juices from the plate.

For 2

belly pork, about 450g, not too lean
4 medium-sized onions
4 garlic cloves
butter, about 50g
bay leaves
flour
a tablespoon of rinsed capers
2 tablespoons grain mustard
a large lemon
chopped parsley

Roast pork

I love to hear the muted crackling of a piece of pork roasting in the oven. A loin or shoulder plonked pink and naked in a tin and roasted will give a palatable result, especially if it sports enough fat to keep it moist. But in practice, a roast of pork only starts to sing when it is seasoned generously with olive oil, garlic and salt. Woody, pungent herbs are a bonus. To smell it, spiked with garlic and sitting on a branch of rosemary, is sheer bliss. There will be rich, succulent meat, sweet fat and golden crackling. That is when it gets sexy. It may be a loin or a shoulder. It may be spiced with anise or herbed with fennel. There may be roast potatoes that have soaked up the fat and juices from the meat and cooked to a crisp, and perhaps a little dish of cooked spinach to one side. I offer two roasts here, a roast loin cooked fast with rosemary and garlic, and a slow-roasted belly spiced in the Chinese manner with aniseed. Both are as easy as can be.

Roast pork with rosemary and garlic

Ask the butcher to score and chine the joint for you; the scoring of the fat induces crisper crackling, the chining – loosening the meat from the backbone – makes for easier carving. Offer a salad of bitter leaves such as rocket, sorrel and chicory afterwards. Watercress will do.

When you arrive home, unwrap the pork loin and season it quite generously with salt and pepper. Rub a small palmful (five or six pinches) into the exposed areas of meat and the meat under the loose backbone. Put in the fridge. It can stay there happily for a few hours.

Set the oven to 220°C/425°F/Gas 7. Put the pork in a shallow, oval dish or roasting tin fat-side up and rubbed with a little olive oil. Nothing fancy, any sort will do. Sprinkle the fat with salt and pepper, at least two or three pinches. Stuff the rosemary and garlic under and around the meat. Dot around a few potatoes or parsnips. Drizzle with a little oil, then roast for 20 minutes. This short burst of high heat will start the process of turning the fat into crisp crackling.

Turn the heat down to 200°C/400°F/Gas 6 and roast for a further fifty minutes. This makes about thirty minutes per half kilo of meat. The meat is pretty much self basting but the vegetables will benefit from a nudge and basting with the pan juices now and again. Don't overdo it, twice will suffice, otherwise the oven heat will be lost. Remove the meat and set to one side. Tip a glass of white wine, anything will do, into the tin. Stir in any tasty-looking bits stuck to the bottom and return the pan and its vegetables to the oven.

After five or six minutes the wine will have made a thin gravy with the pan juices. The vegetables will have crisped, except on the bottom where they will be delectably gooey. Slice the meat, accompany with the vegetables and spoon over the pan juices.

For 4

a piece of pork loin (4 or 5 chops thick), about 1kg, chined and scored by the butcher
olive oil
rosemary, 4 or 5 bushy sprigs
garlic, 3 or 4 fat cloves
2 large potatoes or parsnips, each cut into about 4–6 (there is little point in peeling them)
a glass of white wine

Roast apples

dessert apples, one per person
4 juniper berries per apple, lightly
squashed

Cut each apple round the horizon, going only just deeper than the skin. This will prevent the apple bursting and spilling its fluffy flesh. Put the apples in a baking dish or around the roast about half an hour before the roast is due to come out of the oven. Spoon a few of the pork cooking juices over the fruit, then season with salt, pepper and the crushed juniper berries. Bake till they fluff up, the flesh turning white and frothy.

Crackling

Any celebration of the pig and its meat must mention crackling, that gloriously crisp, golden and chewy layer of skin with melting fat that is so cherished by the British. The French as good as ignore it. The fools. Yet a plate of roast pork is unthinkable without it. And I cannot be the only person who tears a strip of crackling off a cold roast to chew while I read the paper.

There is no great secret, despite what silly people may tell you. Simply get the butcher to score the skin, then rub a little oil and seasoning in it before you put it in the oven. Roast at a high temperature for a while, then turn the heat down a little. No secret.

A celebration of succulence

I rate the meat of the pig above any other. Cured, it is both delicate and highly piquant. A delicacy. Fresh, from an old-fashioned breed that has rooted and snuffled for at least some of its food, it offers gamey meat and sumptuous fat. I itch to use the word scrumptious.

Rich, fatty and succulent, pork is the quintessential autumn and winter meat. Roasted within its coating of fat and crisp skin, it is savoury and sticky. To remove its white fat, softer and more supple than the brittle lamb's, is to take away its heart and soul. To hunt out pork without fat, the pride and joy of some supermarket buyers, is to misunderstand it altogether.

While the presence of fat is what makes this meat so succulent, I suspect it is the varied diet of the free range pig that makes it so interesting. The flavour of the roasted meat of a true farmhouse pig, fed on kitchen scraps, acorns and roots, is richer and more gamey than the bland, white flesh of the depressed and humiliated pig of intensive farming. Roasted with golden parsnips and served with thin gravy, or casseroled with white beans and garlic, pork makes a satisfying meal that needs nothing more than a handful of olives before and a plate of soft-leafed salad after. A slice of ripe pear or silver-grey-skinned fig will suffice as dessert.

Pork can take the pungent notes of the oil-rich, woody herbs, rosemary, sage and thyme. Pork and juniper is a joy; crush the purple-black berries into coarse dust, then mash it into butter to smear a grilled loin chop. But it is the aniseed note of fennel – twiggy herb or icy vegetable – or the more heady star-anise spice that shares a pan most comfortably with the flesh of the pig. Even a careless scattering of tiny, ridged fennel seeds over the meat as it grills should be enough to convince.

Much is made of cooking fruit with pork. Too much. Apples, though, roasted to bursting, lemon, its juice squeezed over the sizzling meat, or a handful of sour Morello cherries, stoned and added to the thin pan gravy, are very flattering. But sourness in the form of sauerkraut or pickled fruits may appeal more. A spoonful of redcurrant jelly melted into the pan juices adds not just piquancy but a shine too.

Pork rises to the piquant; apple sauce, lemon, olives, chicory or juniper. Mustard, too. Such additions do more than cut the meat's inherent richness, they make its flavour sing.

Chops and chicory

For 2

olive oil

butter

2 pork chops, about 225g each,
    loin or rib

a teaspoon of fennel seeds

2 plump heads of white chicory

a wineglass of white wine, ready-
    made vegetable stock or water

Another thirty-minute supper. A 225g chop is about 2.5cm thick and as big as your hand.

You will need a large shallow pan. One to which you have a lid. Pour enough oil into the pan to leave a thin film over the base, about two tablespoons, maybe less. Add a knob of butter, not much bigger than a whole almond, then heat the pan over a moderate flame until the oil starts to sizzle.

Add the chops. Cook on one side till both meat and fat are golden brown, a matter of two or three minutes. They will spit. They will pop. You will need a long-handled fork if you are not to get burned. Season with salt and pepper and scatter a good pinch or two of fennel seeds over the chops and turn them over. Add another pinch. Add the chicory, cut in half lengthways, cut-side down.

Cook until the underside of the chops is golden too, then pour in

the liquid. This can be white wine, vegetable stock or water. Wine gets my vote as the point is to make interestingly flavoured pan juices. Let it come to the boil, then turn down the heat, cover and simmer for about fifteen minutes. Cut into one of the chops; if the flesh is beige then it is done, pink and it is not.

Remove the chops and chicory to warm plates. Leave the juices be. Turn up the heat. Add a further knob of butter to the pan. Not much, about 30g (that's about the size of a walnut). Stir fast, scraping any gooey bits into the melting butter. Tip the golden, bitter, buttery juices immediately over the chops and eat.

» Alternatively, replace the bitterness of the chicory with a butter made from juniper berries, accompanying the chops instead with soft lettuce leaves dressed with the juices from the pan.

Pork rib chops with juniper butter

For 2
a tablespoon/a small palmful of
    juniper berries
50g butter
juice of half a small lemon
2 large pork rib chops
a tablespoon of olive oil

Crush the juniper berries with a pestle and mortar to a coarse powder. They will look like tobacco and smell like gin. Mash in the butter
and the lemon juice and place in the fridge. Deeply score the fat on
the meat several times to stop it curling as it cooks. Warm the oil in a
shallow pan till it shimmers. Add the chops and cook till the underside
is golden brown, about five minutes. Turn and cook the other side for
a similar time. Cut a gash into one of the chops. If the inside is beige
then it is done. Pink, and you should cook it a little longer. Remove to
hot plates.

Add the butter at once to the hot pan and let it partially melt over
the heat, scraping away at the crusty bits and stirring them into the
butter. The savoury crumbs will do wonders for the butter. When it is
foaming in parts but still solid in others, pour the butter quickly over
the chops and accompanying salad, then crumble some sea salt over
with your fingers and eat immediately.

Thai pork rissoles with lime leaves, chillies and mint

Sticky, savoury little cakes, hot with chillies and citrus flavours. I cannot deny that these are simply Thai fish cakes in which I have replaced the fish with pork. As with fish cakes, the texture will be more interesting to eat if you loosely shape them into rough-edged patties rather than attempting perfection. Do not be daunted by the length of the recipe; it is simple and quick.

Mince the fat bacon. This is easiest done in a food processor, although it will actually be very finely chopped rather than minced. At a push you could chop it to a mush by hand – but rather you than me. While the bacon is still in the processor, throw in the spring onions, lime leaves (removing any tough stems), the grated ginger, chilli, garlic and mint. Season generously with both black pepper and salt. Whiz until the aromatics and spices are finely incorporated into the bacon.

Mix with the minced pork and set aside in the cool while the mixture stiffens and the aromatics flavour the meat. For the dipping sauce, bring the rice vinegar and the sugar to the boil in a small saucepan and continue boiling till it turns sticky – a bit like thin golden syrup. Remove from the heat, stir in the soy. Cool, then add the chilli and coriander leaves.

Get a little oil hot in a pan – it doesn't really matter what sort, just enough to cover the bottom in a shallow layer. Shape the seasoned pork into about twelve little patties, burgers if you like, and drop them, half a dozen at a time, into the hot fat.

Fry for a total of ten minutes over a low heat, turning once or twice. They should be cooked right through (test one by breaking it open; it should be light brown, not pink inside) and the surface should be reddy-brown and glistening slightly with stickiness from the bacon fat. Eat immediately with the dipping sauce, dunking each hot, citrus-scented burger into the dip as you eat.

For 3, or 2 very greedy people

125g fatty bacon (such as pancetta)
4 spring onions, roughly chopped
8 large lime leaves
a knob of ginger, about the size of your thumb, grated
a large, hot chilli, chopped
4 cloves of garlic, chopped
a handful of mint leaves, about 12
450g minced pork
a little oil for frying

For the dipping sauce:

5 tablespoons rice vinegar
4 tablespoons sugar
a tablespoon of soy sauce
a small red chilli, seeded and finely chopped
a small handful of coriander leaves, chopped

Sausages

I love a banger. Mild, herby British butcher's variety, blow-your-socks-off fennel and black pepper Italian ones, or thick wodges of black pudding. Love them all.

To be good, really good, a sausage must be hot and sticky. It must sport that tacky, savoury goo that you get when it has been cooked slowly. It must be sweet, savoury, gooey, chewy and all at once. And a sausage should always be eaten when slightly too hot – part of the joy of a banger is to toss it around your mouth while making sucking and blowing noises. A tepid sausage is a friend to no one.

Sausage suppers, whether bangers and mash or grilled black pudding with creamy mustard sauce, are cold-weather food of the first order. I can think of nothing I would rather come in to after raking the leaves on an autumn afternoon than slow-fried sausages and a mountain of mash. Sausage hot pot comes pretty close.

It stands to sense that a sausage will vary in quality more than a joint of meat. There is much room for error and misunderstanding in the mincing room. Frugality has no place in a butcher's shop – least of all in its sausage maker. Save penny-pinching for the faggot recipe. A generous hand with the lean, the fat and the herbs is essential if a banger is to be worth eating. At the risk of upsetting sausage fanciers I honestly think that the plain butcher's sausage is a tastier affair than all these fancy links around at the moment. And I cannot be the only one who prefers a butcher's sausage to the over-garlicked Toulouse jobbies. Give me a ring of fat and freckly Cumberland any day.

Choosing a sausage is not that difficult. But there can be disappointments. Go for butcher's rather than supermarket versions, and choose ones that are meaty and moist-looking, and perhaps freckled with pepper and a few herbs. It is best to avoid the butcher's effort at originality until you have tried their house brand, which may be very good indeed. Some butchers really know how to make a banger. If in doubt, just go for a plump, friendly-looking one – banger, that is.

Sausages with cream and parsley mash

Put the sausages in a large, heavy frying pan over a low heat. Add a little fat to the pan, but only enough to stop them sticking. Lard, oil or dripping is probably best; butter will burn, and marg will ruin a good sausage (or anything else for that matter). Leave the sausages to cook slowly, covered with a lid, turning them once or twice. They will take a good thirty to forty minutes on a slow heat. Patience will be rewarded by a lovely sticky sausage.

Meanwhile, put the potatoes on to boil in salted water. When they are tender, mash them with either a fork or a potato masher. The latter is quicker. Bring the cream to boiling point in a small pan, add the chopped parsley and a good dose of salt and pepper. Pour the hot cream into the mashed potato together with the fat from the cooked sausages. Pile the mash on to plates, the sausages by its side.

For 2

6 butcher's sausages
a little fat, oil or lard
3 large potatoes, peeled
a small pot of double cream
2 handfuls of chopped parsley

Spicy sausages with baked onions in cream

Put the sausages on to cook in a heavy, shallow pan. The heat should be low, the pan covered. Bring a pan of water to the boil, throw in the onions, and let them boil for ten minutes till slightly floppy. Drain and drop them into a thickly buttered shallow baking dish. Pour over the cream (it won't quite cover) and season with salt and pepper (though don't overdo it if the sausages are spicy). Dot a bit more butter on top and bake in a hot oven (200°C/400°F/Gas 6) for about forty minutes till bubbling, the onions a light gold. Turn the sausages from time to time. Serve the onions and their thin, buttery, creamy sauce piping hot, with the sausages and bread to mop.

For 2

6 spicy pork sausages (Italian delis are a good hunting ground)
2 large onions, thickly sliced
a little butter
a small pot of double cream

Bacon

British bacon, particularly when dry-cured rather than soaked in brine, can be worth keeping in the kitchen, even if 'only' for a bacon sandwich eaten in moments of extreme hunger or intoxication. Although good smoked bacon – slightly dry to the touch, dark in colour and heavy with scent of smoke – can be found, it is something of a rarity. Cheesemongers and provincial post offices seem the best bet. The norm seems to be wet, pale and bland, weeping water into the frying pan, ensuring that it steams rather than fries.

With the exception of that bacon sandwich, and the utterly delicious liver and bacon, I tend to use bacon rashers quite rarely. They become irreplaceable to the cook when grilled crisply and snipped into a spinach and avocado salad, wrapped around scallops and grilled or when included with the sausage, fried bread and mushrooms of the famous British breakfast.

Prosciutto

I can think of no more successful appetiser than little scraps of prosciutto, cut thick and with their fat attached, laid unadorned on a white plate. Scraps that are savoury and sweet at once. Scraps that tease and delight. Yet cured meats have starred in many a more substantial meal in my house. A summer lunch with tiny purple olives, a lump of white bread from a new loaf and a pear that I can eat at my desk; the point of a plate of salad, torn into strips and tossed with spicy rocket, mild, milky Taleggio and sliced marinated artichokes, or simply stuffed into a wedge of ciabatta with a cheeky gherkin.

By prosciutto I mean the rear thigh of the pig that has been salted and dried. Boar, beef and birds are also cured but are not as readily available. Methods vary, breeds vary, quality varies. Beg at your delicatessen, in a quiet moment, for morsels to taste; including the mild, pale prosciutto di Parma, the darker, sweet jamón serrano from Spain or the French jambon de Bayonne, which is lightly smoked. My favourite cures are dark, chewy and salty. Though I would not say no to a delicate, pale, fragrant slice to wrap around a halved fig or slice of pear. As long as it was cut thicker than is the tendency.

Prosciutto is in high spirits when it appears alongside sweet, tender, juicy fruits, in particular peaches, figs and yellow- or apricot-fleshed melons. Serve as a salad with the fruits cut into segments, catching their juice over the serving plate.

There is little to be gained from cooking such delicacies as prosciutto, though I have enjoyed a fillet of red mullet (Franco Taruschio at the Walnut Tree Inn in Wales) and a turkey steak (the recipe appears in my earlier book, *The 30-Minute Cook*) wrapped in a slice of Parma ham and fried. The ham seasoned, moistened and added clout to the dishes. But if I am going to cook with cured meat then I would generally rather use pancetta.

Prosciutto and pears

Tear each slice of ham into two long strips, slice the pear, which should be so ripe as to dribble when cut, into quarters and remove the core. Wrap the ham around the slices of pear and eat straight away. The more savoury the ham and the more luscious the pear, the better.

For 1
2 large, thin slices of prosciutto
1 very ripe, juicy pear

Pancetta

Herby, spicy, perfumed pancetta is the air-dried belly of the pig, the same cut we use for streaky bacon. Eat it raw, in tissue-thin slices with pears or melon, as you might prosciutto di Parma. One sniff of its sweet, milky fat, cured with fennel seeds, nutmeg and garlic, transports me to the dark, cool, backstreet delicatessens of Florence or Venice. I use it in preference to bacon for wrapping quail or guinea fowl before roasting; its aromatic fat moistening and seasoning the bird with more discretion than bacon.

Bought in the piece, rather than in transparent slices, it can be diced to form the basis of a *soffritto*, the diced onion, carrot and garlic mixture that is the starting point for many Italian slow-cooked dishes. Pan-fried in its own fat till crisp, it is an agreeable addition to a plate of frilly green and white frisée, especially when the liquid fat from the pan becomes, with the addition of a dash of wine vinegar, the dressing.

If pancetta eludes you, which it may well without easy access to a decent supermarket or deli, the answer is to use streaky bacon. But it is, of course, a less aromatic, less fragrant, less interesting answer.

Pan-fried potatoes with pancetta and parsley

You can do a version with any old bacon but it will be less aromatic than if you use pancetta.

Cut the pancetta into small cubes, about the size of dolly mixtures. Maybe a little bigger. Put them in a large, shallow pan, one to which you have a lid, and cook them over a moderate flame until their fat runs. Cut the potatoes into slightly larger cubes (you can peel them if the skin bothers you) and add them to the pan. Fry till they start to spit and sizzle, then cover them. Leave to cook until the potatoes are tender, about twenty minutes, shaking the pan from time to time.

Remove the lid and turn up the heat. Add a couple of glugs of olive oil. Fry the potatoes, prising them gently from the pan with a spatula, till golden. Throw in the parsley. Taste the potatoes. They will be golden brown, crumbly and stuck to the pan. Eat while hot.

» An exceptionally savoury supper can be made by doing nothing more than covering the above, still in the pan, with thin slices of Gruyère, Cantal, fontina or Cheddar and grilling till the cheese starts to ooze and melt. A beer would be appropriate here.

For 2
175g pancetta, in the piece
2 large (but not huge) potatoes, any type
olive oil
a handful of chopped parsley

Lamb
& Other Meats

Lamb is the only meat in which the seasons still have their say. But flavour is on the side of the patient, and those who can wait till summer will be rewarded with more succulence and flavour than those who insist on paying through the nose for the first spring lamb. They only do it for show. They surely cannot do it for flavour. By late summer, lamb is worthy of its reputation as the favourite meat for feasting, though I am not one to do battle with a whole animal on a spit.

Yet a lamb chop can be a feast. That is, if the fat is crisp, the meat lightly charred and smoky outside and pink and juicy within. Held by its hot, brittle bone, its pink juices dribbling down fingers and chin, it is a feast in every sense of the word. Of course the fibres get wedged between your teeth, but the licking of lips and sucking of teeth is one of the joys of eating. Unless you are a prude at the table. But that is your business and loss.

Lamb is the sweetest of meats, and most cuts will roast, grill or fry. I have on occasion thrown a leg of lamb in the oven without fat or seasoning and it has come out tender and tasty. This meat is naturally moist, and rarely suffers from the dryness that can afflict a piece of beef or pork. But its fat has few fans. I devour it with unconcealed relish when it frames a grilled lamb cutlet, offering a crisp contrast to the melting meat. But the meat is the point.

Lamb's Christmas card list is a long one but an economical version might include garlic, thyme, tomatoes, more garlic and Beaujolais. Some would say mint. Others not. Onions, orange and rosemary are flattering when used with discretion. Try adding them to a roast or a more traditional casserole. Although I am unsure as to the point of the cream-enriched lamb stews such as the French *blanquette d'agneau,* I can think of few more sublime accompaniments to roast lamb than a garlicky potato gratin. Especially when the juices from the lamb mingle on the plate with the creamy, garlic sauce from the gratin. Then there are little surprises such as the anchovies that you can bury in the fat of a roasting leg (poke them in with a skewer) or the aubergines you can roast alongside a shoulder. Not to mention the balsamic vinegar used to enrich the pan juices of a grilled lamb chop.

Shepherd's pie with spiced parsnip mash

Buttery, spiced mash and herby, mushroomy minced lamb – a one-dish meal for friends. Cooking the onions till they are golden and sweet will make the world of difference to the flavour. As will the slow cooking of the meat sauce.

Cut the parsnips into large chunks and simmer them in salted water until tender, about fifteen to twenty minutes. While they are cooking fry the onions in the butter over a moderate heat until soft and translucent. Stir in the spices and continue cooking for two minutes till all is fragrant. Drain the parsnips when they are tender, mash them with a potato masher, stirring in the butter and some salt and black pepper, then the spiced onions. Set aside.

In a large pan, cook the chopped leeks or onions and the diced carrot with the dripping or butter (enough that when melted it covers the bottom of the pan), until they are meltingly soft and golden. If they have caught slightly at the edges then all to the good. This is the savoury base on which you are making your pie filling, so it is best not to hurry. Add the sliced mushrooms and cook for a further five minutes, then stir in the minced meat. The meat must brown a little here and there, so do not stir it too often. Leave to cook for five minutes or so, breaking it up as necessary.

Add a casual sprinkling of flour (about a tablespoon) and the tomato purée. Continue to cook, stirring regularly, for three or four minutes. Tomato purée is bitter if not thoroughly cooked. Pour on the hot stock, throw in a bay leaf and a sprig of thyme if you have them, and bring to the boil. Turn down the heat and leave to simmer very gently for a good twenty-five minutes. The mixture should not really bubble, just occasionally 'bloop' at you. Season the filling as it cooks with salt, Worcestershire sauce (about a tablespoon) and a few grinds of black pepper. Be generous.

Scoop the mixture into a large baking dish. Spoon dollops of mashed parsnip over the top, and bake for twenty-five minutes at 190°C/375°F/Gas 5, till golden brown and caught a little on the peaks.

For 4 generously

900g large parsnips, peeled
2 medium-sized onions, sliced
a thick slice, about 50g, butter
a large pinch of ground cumin
a teaspoon of freshly ground
    coriander seeds
a tablespoon of garam masala
more butter for mashing, about
    50g

For the filling:

2 medium-sized leeks or onions,
    chopped
a medium-sized carrot, diced
3 heaped tablespoons of dripping
    or a thick slice of butter
4 medium-sized brown
    mushrooms, sliced
450g minced roast lamb or raw
    lamb mince
flour
a tablespoon tomato purée
250ml hot stock (a cube will do)
a bay leaf and a sprig of thyme
Worcestershire sauce

Lamb chops with Marsala

For 2
olive oil
2 lamb chops cut from the chump
    end, about 2cm thick, 150g
    each
Marsala

Marsala, the dark, sweet Italian wine that I am tempted to describe as sherry meets port, is an unusual partner for lamb. Yet it works better than I thought it would when I reached for the bottle. One of the joys of being a broad-minded cook. (I might add it hasn't all been roses.) But lamb takes both sweet and acid in its stride, and is as happy sharing a plate with sweet roasted red peppers as with a tart grilled tomato.

Put some olive oil in a frying or sauté pan over a high heat. A tablespoon or two will suffice. When it is hot put in the chops. They will sizzle and spit. Cook for two minutes, then lower the heat and cover with a lid. Leave undisturbed for two minutes, then lift and peep. The fat should be golden, the flesh an appetising brown in patches. A sticky

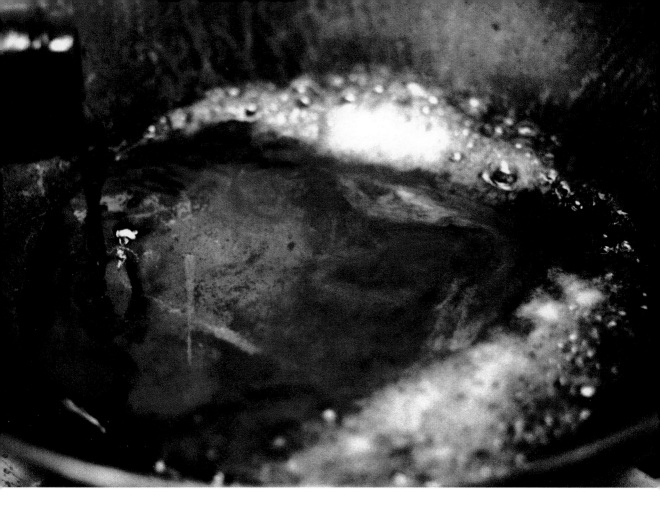

goo should be starting to form in the pan. Treasure it – it's the point of your sauce. Turn the chops over and cook the other side till that too is brown, about a further two minutes. Any longer and they will lose their joy. They must be pink in the middle if they are to be good. Remove the chops to a warm plate. Pour away most of the oil. Turn up the heat and pour in a little Marsala. About an egg cup full, maybe a little less. Now scrape away at all the crusty, sticky, brown goo and golden bits on the bottom of the pan, stirring them into the Marsala. Leave to bubble for a minute. It will start to shine. Pour the sauce over the chops – it will be thin and intensely flavoured – and eat immediately, seasoned with a little crumbled sea salt and a few grinds from the pepper mill. Green beans on the side and bread to mop up the juices.

Shish kebab with mint and pitta

For 2

2 handfuls of flat-leaf parsley
a handful (about 30) mint leaves
2 cloves of garlic, squashed
a tablespoon of grain mustard
a tablespoon of capers, rinsed
juice of a lemon
4 tablespoons olive oil (nothing
    fancy)
350g lamb (shoulder, loin or leg),
    cut into rough cubes, about as
    big as a walnut in its shell
olive oil

To serve:

2 pitta bread, warmed and split
2 handfuls of salad leaves –
    lettuce, rocket, frisée,
    whatever

Any cooking method that creates a dark, savoury crust while allowing the flesh inside to stay pink is right for lamb. In other words, grilling or frying rather than poaching or stewing. The zenith for this meat may well be the shish kebab, its rough cubes of meat cooked scorched and salty over glowing coals, then stuffed into a pocket of comforting pitta bread. I find it hard to think of lamb I have enjoyed more than the street kebabs of Greece and Turkey, made, no doubt, from hillside lamb that has had to work for its meagre grass. Our jaws may have to work harder too.

Whiz the parsley, mint, garlic, mustard, capers and lemon juice in the food processor, adding the oil gradually till all is reduced to a thick sludge. The sort of thing you find at the bottom of a pond. Set aside.

Toss the lamb with a generous amount of salt and finely ground black pepper and a little of the mint dressing. Thread the cubes of lamb on to skewers but do not pack the chunks too close to one another. Get the grill pan or griddle hot (and I mean hot – you should be able to feel the heat rising when you hold your hand a few inches above it), then put the skewers on the pan. Press them down till they spit and pop.

Turn the heat down slightly and cook until the meat is brown in some places, lightly charred and crisp in others. Three, perhaps four minutes, then turn and cook the other side. Slice into a cube of lamb. It is ready when lightly scorched outside, juicy and pink within. Remove from the skewers with a fork, toss quickly with the rest of the dressing, then stuff into the warm pitta with the salad.

Grilled lamb with balsamic vinegar

Rub the lamb with a little olive oil – just enough to make it wet and shiny. Scatter a couple of good pinches of *herbes de Provence* over each side, then set aside for a few minutes. Get a cast iron grill pan hot, put the lamb down on the bars of the grill pan and press down with a palette knife. Let the meat cook for three minutes, then turn. It should be brown with darker lines across it. Season with salt and quite coarsely ground pepper, then cook for a further three minutes. It will be pink inside. Brown and savoury on the outside, with smart black lines from the grill. Shake a few drops of balsamic vinegar over the cooked lamb but don't drown it. Eat while it is hot, with green salad to mop up the fabulous juices that ooze from the meat as you cut it, and perhaps some potatoes. Dauphinoise would be just about perfect if you have the time.

For 2

2 lamb steaks, a good 3cm thick
 and each about 180g in weight
olive oil
herbes de Provence
balsamic vinegar

Lean and young and very well-hung

There is a purity to lamb that may appeal to those suspicious of the practices of intensive farming. Sheep demand little attention from the farmer, despite the image of the shepherd and his flock. That shepherd may have nursed the young lambs and wrapped them in a blanket made from the soft wool of their parents but we all know what he probably had for his supper. The sight of black-faced, jelly-limbed lambs gambolling in the fields does nothing to lessen our taste for this, the most tender of meats.

I have no time for the much-prized meat of young sheep, slaughtered at about six weeks and labelled 'milk lamb'. It is an overrated mouthful, offering interest to neither teeth nor taste-buds. But such mild-flavoured, soft-textured flesh will probably appeal to those who find joy in a veal escalope.

Once past its first flush of youth, the meat of the lamb has more to say. Deep pink, almost brown in colour, the flesh benefits from the grass diet denied to rose-hued milk lamb, and makes for richer eating. As the animal ages into mutton, its flavour gets stronger. Lucky the shoppers who can lay their hands on it.

Lamb rarely eats tough, in the way pork or beef can, even

the oldest animal being worth eating. A lean mountain sheep, its life spent climbing for thin, tough grass and hillside herbs, makes the most flavoursome of roasts. A sheep that has barely looked up from its constant munching of lush downland pastures may be more tender, though.

Most of us get our lamb cradled in blue Styrofoam trays from the supermarket, complete with a little white nappy to soak up any leaks. This meat is often less interesting than that from the butcher, who may have hung his lamb a little longer, perhaps for a week or more, improving both tenderness and flavour. I make a point, contrary to everything I have ever read, of looking out for dark-fleshed, well hung, red-brown butcher's lamb. The sort you see in butcher's shops in Greece. If you can find it for flies.

Fat – sticky and rich – is the bonus for the pork eater. With lamb it is the bones. The sweet, crunchy, brittle bones of a cutlet, or the softer lump in a chump chop, are a true treat for those not too proud to gnaw at the table. Lamb clings to its bones more tightly than does pork or beef, demanding that we pick up and chew. The meat around the bone being the sweetest of course. Cutlery is for wimps.

Braised lamb

I used to think lamb was at its best only when flung on a glowing grill and cooked until the outside was charred and the inside remained pink. The way I have eaten it in Morocco and Greece, spiked with cumin and chopped mint. Despite a soft-spot for a roasted shoulder or leg, for me, lamb was the quintessential high-heat quick-cook meat. My butcher changed all that. I had gone shopping for a fatty, bony piece of pork to cook slowly with wine and beans but was out of luck. A cut of lamb from the middle neck (fat to enrich the sauce and bones to gnaw later) was suggested. Later I discovered the lamb shanks – sweet meat and melting fat – that proved a perfect contender for a sticky and unctuous pot for a cold night.

Moroccan spiced lamb shanks
with aubergine

A lazy, one-pot dish that cooks pretty much all by itself. The preparation is easy and quick, the rest requiring nothing more from the cook than patience. Once you have eaten all the meat, the brick-red glop makes a good soup or pasta sauce. Like so much of this sort of slow-cooked food, it tastes even better the next day.

Dust the lamb shanks with flour and brown them on all sides in the olive oil. Just enough to coat the bottom of the pan. You might as well do this in the same pan you will cook them in (it will save washing up and some of the flavour might adhere usefully to the bottom) – a large casserole is best. Remove the lamb and pour in more oil, add the chunks of aubergine and brown lightly on both sides, adding more oil as the aubergine soaks it up. Lift out and add to the lamb.

Lower the heat slightly and add the onions and garlic, adding more oil if necessary. Cook until pale golden and translucent. As they cook, the onions will soak up the tasty lamb sediment stuck to the pan. Add the tomato purée, harissa paste and cinnamon and cook for another couple of minutes. Tip in the chopped tomatoes and return the lamb and aubergine to the pan. Add salt, say a half teaspoon, and enough water to bring the mixture almost to the top of the shanks. Bring to the boil, then cover and cook in a low oven (170°C/325°F/Gas 3) for about two hours, until all is an aromatic, tender slop, the meat almost falling from the bone. (After about an hour and a half's cooking you should remove the lid and scoop the orange oil from the surface with a large spoon.) This cut being what it is, cooking times will vary, and it may need thirty minutes more.

Remove from the oven, lift the meat out on to a dish and simmer the juices on the hob until all is slushy, the flavour concentrated. Taste and correct the seasoning with salt, pepper and harissa.

Serve hot, as it is, with spoons and bread for the sauce.

For 2

2 small lamb shanks
a little flour
olive oil
a large aubergine, halved
    lengthways and thickly sliced
3 medium-sized onions, sliced
3 plump cloves of garlic, sliced
a heaped tablespoon of tomato
    purée
2 teaspoons harissa paste
a stick of cinnamon
a medium tin (400g) of chopped
    tomatoes

Italian-style slow-cooked aromatic lamb

For 2

a good cupful of dried beans such
    as cannellini (about 300g)
4 middle neck chops, about
    6–7cm thick
a medium-sized onion, cut into
    segments
bay leaves, a few sprigs of thyme
celery, a stalk or two, sliced
carrots, a couple, sliced
3 cloves of garlic, squashed
a large dried chilli, or 2 small
an orange
a bottle of red wine – anything
    drinkable will do
olive oil or dripping
a couple of large, flat brown
    mushrooms, quartered
a tablespoon of balsamic vinegar

A dark and sticky braise. No fuss – just throw the ingredients first into wine overnight, then into a pot to bubble slowly.

Soak the beans in cold water overnight. Put the lamb, onion, herbs, celery, carrots, garlic and chilli and a few peppercorns in a china or glass dish. Peel off a good length of orange peel with a potato peeler and add to the dish with the remainder of the orange, sliced. Pour over enough red wine to cover the meat. Set aside overnight, somewhere cool, though it need not be the fridge.

Drain the beans, bring them to the boil in a pot of water, then boil hard for about fifteen minutes. Cover and turn off the heat. Melt a large knob of dripping, enough to cover the bottom of a heavy-based casserole, one to which you have a lid. When it starts to sizzle, lift the lamb out of its marinade and add to the pan. Leave for a minute or two until it is brown on one side. Turn it over and brown the other. Lift out with a draining spoon, then add the remaining ingredients from the marinade and the mushrooms. Cook for a good ten minutes or until they have softened. They will probably have stuck to the bottom – which is to the good.

Pour in the wine from the marinade plus the rest of the bottle and then add the drained beans. Bring to the boil over a medium heat, turning it down just before it actually boils. Add the balsamic vinegar and the lamb, cover the pot with greaseproof paper (an extra device to stop the liquid evaporating) and a lid. Leave to simmer gently, at a lazy bubble, for about an hour and a half. Check the meat for tenderness – it should be tender enough to fall easily from the bone. The beans should squash easily against the side of the pan.

Turn up the heat and cook at a vigorous bubble, uncovered, until the cooking juices have thickened slightly – a matter of ten to fifteen minutes, carefully watched. Taste the liquid, it may need salt, and possibly a few grinds of pepper. Serve hot, in deep bowls or soup plates, with hunks of bread and a bottle of wine.

Leg of lamb with garlic and rosemary, with potatoes baked in the juices from the roast

For 6

6 large potatoes, scrubbed
olive oil, not much
butter, about 50g
a leg of lamb (about 2kg in
    weight)
a few bushy sprigs of rosemary
6 cloves of garlic, peeled

Slice the potatoes without bothering to peel them. They should be not much thicker than a pound coin. Lay them in a roasting tin and drizzle over a little oil, then add the butter in small pieces and a shaking of salt.

Set the oven to 230°C/450°F/Gas 8. Pierce the fat of the leg of lamb with the point of a sharp knife. Into each hole stuff a small sprig of rosemary and a slice of garlic (do the rosemary first, it makes it easier to get the garlic in). Drizzle and dab both fat and aromatics with olive oil. Grind over a little salt and set the joint on one of the oven shelves. Place the roasting tin of potatoes underneath (directly underneath or you will have to clean the oven afterwards) and leave to roast for about fifteen minutes per 500g, in other words about an hour. After twenty minutes, turn the oven temperature down to 200°C/400°F/Gas 6. During cooking, the juices from the lamb will drip over the potatoes – rendering them both crunchy and soft, and soaked in flavour.

Remove the lamb from the oven and let it settle for ten minutes before carving. While the lamb rests, turn the oven up again to crisp the potatoes. Serve the lamb with the potatoes. I am not sure you need anything else.

Offal – the wobbly, knobbly bits

There is something slightly perverted about enjoying offal. Creamy, jelly-tender sweetbreads, silky, melt-in-your-mouth liver and juicy kidneys of the lamb are something to be wolfed in private by those in the know. (Lamb's liver with onion gravy and parsnip mash is utter bliss to me.) I count myself as an offal fancier, though even I cannot get it up for slippery, slithery sheets of tripe. But I do buy a heart now and again for the cat.

Offal is a secret to be shared, and the biggest secret of all is lamb's sweetbreads. I urge you to try them. They have not done anything horrid, and are nothing more than the pancreas and thymus glands. Which should please the squeamish. Their flesh is the tenderest on the animal and truly deserves the epithet melting. You can sauté them with booze and cream, or serve them with a punchy salsa verde. If you are an offal missionary, trying to convert those you love to the delights of guts and stuff, then you may find that, crumbed and fried, the sweetbread is easiest for them to cope with. Especially if you fail to tell them what it is.

Of course, this is boy's food, all these entrails and stuff. Offal has become the modern-day equivalent of the vindaloo. It is now less a case of how hot a curry you can tolerate, more how grizzly a gland you can devour. But offal is also autumn food. It was eaten first when the animals were slaughtered for winter. You cannot preserve offal like you can the other cuts. The rich flavours of these bits go with the foods of the season, mushrooms, vinegar, mashed potatoes and mustard.

Pan-fried sweetbreads with anchovy butter

Preparing sweetbreads involves soaking, skinning and generally fiddling around. In my book it's a butcher's job. I suggest you buy your sweetbreads ready prepared.

Rinse the sweetbreads thoroughly and pat dry on kitchen paper. Chop the anchovies and mash them with the lemon juice and almost all of the butter. A pestle and mortar is the job for this. But a bowl and spoon will work. Stir in the parsley and a little finely ground black pepper. No salt.

Melt the remaining butter in a shallow pan. When it starts to bubble and fizz, add the sweetbreads and cook over high heat for three minutes, turning the breads over once and cooking for a further three minutes till they are golden brown in patches. Transfer to warm plates, tip out the butter and add the anchovy butter to the pan. Bring to the boil, scraping the bottom of the pan with a wooden spoon as you do so. Pour the warm anchovy butter over the sweetbreads and serve. Boiled potatoes and green beans or salad accompany.

For 2

350g lamb's sweetbreads, soaked and skinned
8 fat, juicy anchovy fillets, drained and patted dry
juice of half a lemon
100g butter, at room temperature
a small handful of chopped parsley

Lamb's liver with red wine vinegar and sticky onions

For 2

3 medium-sized onions

a thick slice/50g butter and a little more for the liver

a tablespoon of olive oil

enough buttery mashed potatoes for 2 (page 250)

about 350g lamb's liver, thinly sliced

3 tablespoons red wine vinegar

The quicker liver is cooked, the more melting it is likely to be. Once its heart has changed from red to pinky-brown it is not worth eating.

Get the onions on first, then the mash. The liver takes seconds.

Peel the onions and then cut each of them into six segments from stalk to tip. Cook them slowly, over a low heat, in the butter and oil. You need not cover them, or stir them very often, but you should have the patience to let them soften and colour for at least half an hour. Stirring too often prevents the lovely, sticky goo adhering to the pan – frankly the whole point of the dish. By which time they should be sweet and slightly sticky. Scoop out the onions, cover and keep them warm.

Melt a walnut-sized knob of butter in the onion pan. You need not wipe the pan. In fact it is better if you do not. When the butter sizzles furiously, add the liver. Do not move the slices until they are golden brown in patches, about a minute, maybe two, then turn them over and cook for a further minute. Remove the liver to warm plates. Overcooking it is embarrassingly easy.

Throw the red wine vinegar into the pan, letting it sizzle and splutter. Scrape at any sticky goo in the pan until it dislodges itself, add a little salt and some black pepper, then stir it into the juices. Pour the contents of the pan over the liver. Serve immediately with the mash and onions. Of course, the real joy of this supper is mashing the potatoes and onions into the vinegar gravy.

Other meats

I eat meat about twice a week. While I find chicken, pork and lamb the most rewarding to cook with, other tastes beckon from time to time – the strident flavour of game in autumn (for which you should turn to the chicken chapter), or perhaps the mild meat of a rabbit with herbs for a summer Sunday lunch. And although I have never had a taste for beef, once in a blue moon I do get the urge for a grilled steak, all served up with golden *frites* and a piquant pool of béarnaise sauce. It is a bit of a palaver. Worth it, though.

Steak and chips with béarnaise sauce

For 2
2 rump or sirloin steaks, about
   200g each
a little olive oil
hot French fries (see page 244)
   to serve

The béarnaise sauce:
3 tablespoons white wine vinegar
a shallot, chopped
6 black peppercorns
a teaspoon of dried tarragon
   leaves
2 egg yolks
a teaspoon of Dijon mustard
150g soft, almost melted, butter
a palmful of chopped tarragon
   leaves

There is less expertise needed in cooking a juicy, delectably savoury steak than we are led to believe. You need a hot grill and a thick slice of well-hung rump (forget fillet, it's overpriced and not half as tasty). And the béarnaise sauce is a doddle. Get the chips through their first frying before you make the sauce, then give them their second cooking while the steak is grilling.

For the sauce put the vinegar, chopped shallot, peppercorns and dried tarragon leaves into a small saucepan (not aluminium) with two tablespoons of water. Bring to the boil and simmer until there is very little liquid left. This will take almost no time at all. There should be just a few dregs in the bottom of the pan.

Put the egg yolks into a heatproof glass or china bowl and sit it over a pan of simmering water. Working quickly, add the mustard. The base of the bowl should not quite touch the water. Pour the tarragon and vinegar mixture into the egg yolks and mustard, holding the solids back with a spoon, and whisk gently. Add the butter, a little at a time, whisking gently between each addition. The sauce will thicken. Keep whisking in the butter until the mixture is thick and creamy. Stir in the chopped tarragon and a little salt.

The sauce should be as thick as custard. If it shows any sign of thickening or going grainy (and it well might), then pour in a little boiling water and whisk furiously for a minute. It will come back together. You can keep it warm, over the pan of (switched-off) water, whisking occasionally, while you grill the steak.

For the steak: how you like your steak cooked is your business. But I might suggest that it is not worth eating unless it has some juice inside. For which of course you can read blood. Once a steak is brown all the way through it becomes a dull chew. I find the best results involve using one of those ridged cast-iron grill pans that sit over the gas; the meat catching on the ridges in thin, black, crispy stripes.

Get the grill pan hot, you should be able to feel the heat when you hold your hand over it. It will take about four minutes to come up to heat over a moderate flame. To test it, splash a few drops of water over it. They should pop and disappear immediately.

Oil the steak on both sides, put the meat on the grill pan and leave well alone for at least a full minute. Do not move it. Press it down on the bars of the grill pan with a palette knife. If your steak is about 1.75cm thick, and it probably will be, then you should leave it for two minutes, turn it over, season it with salt and black pepper, then cook for a further two minutes. Test the steak with your finger, it should have a slight bounce to it. You can cut into it if you wish, but you are only letting all the juices out. If you want it more brown than pink, then cook it a minute or two longer. Season as you put it on the plate (which should be warm; steak goes cold quickly). Eat with béarnaise and chips.

Rabbit with cream and mustard

A mild, creamy, sleepy sort of dish for the days when you want something to soothe rather than dazzle. It works just as well with chicken.

Mash together the garlic and mustard with a seasoning of salt and a few grinds from the pepper mill. Stir in enough olive oil to make a thin paste. About two or three glugs. Rub the mixture all over the rabbit pieces. Place them in a shallow baking dish, drizzle over a little more olive oil and bake at 190°C/375°F/Gas 5 for about twenty-five minutes.

Remove the dish from the oven and pour off most of the oil. Tip the cream over the rabbit, stirring it into the remaining oil and mixing in the mustard, spooning and smearing it over the rabbit. Continue to bake for a further twenty minutes or until the rabbit is golden and crusty. Shake the dish to bring the sauce together, stirring if you need to, then serve hot, with bread and perhaps green beans.

For 2
3 cloves of garlic, peeled
2 tablespoons French mustard
    (preferably one of Dijon and
    one of grain mustard)
olive oil
4 rabbit joints, to include 2 legs
small pot (about 150ml) double
    cream

Pasta, Beans, Rice & Grains

A plate of pasta can soothe or startle. Bathed in cream and cheese it will send us to sleep. Spiked with chilli it will make our heart beat faster and our noses run. Pasta is the quintessential mood food. And the choice is up to the cook.

I make pasta once a year in a messy, unprofessional way. I am mysteriously proud of the uneven, slimy, chewy results. For the other fifty-one weeks of the year I buy the dried stuff. Any shape except spaghetti, which I find infuriating to eat. I am especially fond of the cup, nib and shell shapes that hold such generous quantities of sauce. Less fond of the ribbons that one has to wind around the fork. I am an impatient eater.

The common or garden Italian dried pasta made with hard wheat and egg is often interchangeable with the less well-known soft-flour oriental noodles. But while Japanese noodles seasoned in an unorthodox fashion with garlic, basil and Parmesan cheese is better than no supper at all, it will feel strange in the mouth. Somehow not quite right. Perversely, soy sauce, chillies and black beans seem to work perfectly well with firm Italian pastas.

Playing around at the weekend with cheese sauce, layers of velvety spinach lasagne and rich meat sauce can be fun. But for me, pasta will always remain the once-a-week 'what-the-hell-can-we-eat-tonight?' supper. That is not to put it down. If

anything it is to extol its virtue of usefulness. Fondness, perhaps, rather than respect.

Dried egg pasta takes about ten minutes to cook. Chinese noodles about four. Check its progress continually. It is ready when it is as you like it. Despite what it may say on the packet and what the experts say, the texture of cooked pasta is a personal thing. Most people tend to prefer it cooked till tender but far from soft – in other words until it still has a bit of bite left in it. But cook it to suit you and whoever else you are cooking for – rather than be pushed around by purist opinion. It is your supper, after all.

This is also the chapter in which you will find the warming, homely grains, the couscous and the beany casseroles, the creamy risottos, spicy pilafs and the crisp, garlicky bean fritters. The comfort food pages.

Soothing, creamy pasta

Pasta with spicy sausage and mustard

For 2
4 spicy Italian pork sausages
olive oil
4 handfuls of dried pasta (any
    tube or shell shape), about
    250g
a glass of white wine
dried chilli flakes, a pinch or two
a small handful of chopped basil
a tablespoon of Dijon mustard
200ml double cream

Spicy, hot and creamy. Pasta for a cold night.

Put a large pan of water on to boil for the pasta. Split the sausages open and take out the filling. Warm a little olive oil in a frying pan, just enough to lubricate the bottom. Discard the sausage skins, crumble the meat into the hot pan and fry till sizzling and cooked through, about five minutes. Salt the water and add the pasta.

Pour the wine into the sausage pan and let it bubble a little, scraping at the sausage goo stuck to the bottom of the pan. Stir in the chilli flakes and chopped basil. Add a little salt and the mustard, pour in the cream and bring slowly to a simmer. Cook for a minute or two, stirring now and again.

When the pasta is tender, about nine minutes after coming back to the boil, drain and tip into the creamy sausage sauce. Serve piping hot.

Pasta with caramelised onions, basil and cream

For 2, or 4 as a side dish
2 large onions, peeled
4 garlic cloves, thinly sliced
butter, about 50g
olive oil
Madeira, Marsala or balsamic
    vinegar
200ml double cream
pasta, any shape, for 2 (about
    300g)
a handful of chopped basil

A rich, sweet pasta dish, particularly suitable for serving as a side dish to grilled lamb or chicken.

Cut the onions into segments from shoot to root, about eight from each one. Cook them with the garlic in a lump of butter, about as big as a walnut, and just enough olive oil to cover the bottom of the pan. Cook over a low to moderate heat, stirring very occasionally, until the onions are completely soft and golden. This will take a full twenty minutes, if not longer. As they are the point of the sauce, it is worth taking some care over them. Ideally they will be soft enough to crush between your fingers.

Put a large pan of water on to boil for the pasta. Cook the pasta until tender, about nine minutes or so for dried pasta, depending on how soft you like it. Whatever you do, don't cook it for more than eleven. Meanwhile, turn the heat up a little under the onions so that

they become a rich brown at the edges. Overcooking will send them bitter. Pour in a few splashes from the Madeira or Marsala bottle, or if you have neither a few generous glugs of balsamic vinegar, leave to almost evaporate, then pour in the cream and scatter the basil into the onions, simmer gently at a low bubble for a couple of minutes, then season with salt and pepper. Drain the pasta, toss with the sauce and eat while still hot.

Baked pasta with aubergine, cream and garlic

For 2

2 large handfuls of dried pasta, about 150g
a medium-sized aubergine, halved lengthways
olive oil
3 cloves of garlic, thinly sliced
2 medium-sized tomatoes, sliced
a generous handful of basil leaves, torn up a little
about 300ml double cream
a lump of Parmesan cheese

Cream and aubergines are a successful clash of cultures, ensuring the most voluptuous of textures. The cream will not entirely cover the pasta, but no matter. Be generous with the basil leaves.

Cook the pasta in boiling, salted water till tender, about ten minutes. Drain. Cut the aubergine into slices about as thick as a pound coin, maybe a little thicker. Fry the aubergine slices, a few at a time, in olive oil in a shallow pan till soft and golden. You may have to top up the oil level, which should just cover the bottom of the pan, from time to time. Add the sliced garlic with the last batch of aubergine. Mix the drained pasta, fried aubergine slices, garlic, tomatoes, basil and cream. Season with salt and black pepper.

Tip into a large ovenproof dish. A large gratin dish or even a small roasting tin will do. Grate enough Parmesan over the top to make a thin layer. Bake in a hot oven at 200°C/400°F/Gas 6 until bubbling (about twenty-five minutes), the cheese slightly golden. Serve with a few green salad leaves to mop up the oily, creamy, garlicky juices on the plate.

Pasta with prosciutto and Parmesan cream sauce

For 2

any dried pasta (ribbon, tube or shell) for two (about 275g/ 4 big handfuls)
a large knob of butter, about 30g
prosciutto, sliced, about 75g
150ml double cream
a handful of grated Parmesan cheese

Sexy, savoury, soothing. For when you are in one of 'those' moods.

Drop the pasta into a large pan of boiling, salted water and let it cook at a vigorous bubble until tender but firm – probably about ten minutes but check its progress from about eight. Drain, not too thoroughly, so that there is a little water left clinging to the pasta – it will help the consistency of the sauce.

Five minutes before you expect the pasta to be ready, melt the butter in a shallow pan. Slice the prosciutto finely, or tear it into shreds, then fry it in the butter for a minute. It will darken a little. Pour in the cream, bring to the boil, then add the cheese. Let the sauce bubble a few times, then add the pasta to it. Tip into a warm bowl and serve.

Light, fresh-tasting pasta

Pasta with lemon, green herbs and toasted crumbs

Any fresh herbs will work here with the exception of the robust varieties such as spiky rosemary or tough, old thyme. Choose just two or three varieties rather than a confusing mixture of anything you can lay your hands on, and try to make a balance of flavours, such as one handful of aniseed-flavoured herbs like chervil, tarragon or fennel and one of peppery basil. A few chives would be welcome, though not in an overpowering quantity.

Put a large pan of water on to boil. Salt it and when it comes to the boil add the pasta. Cook for nine minutes, or until tender with a little bite left to it. Meanwhile pour a little olive oil into a frying pan, just enough to cover the bottom, and get it hot. Add the garlic and the crumbs, then turn the heat down and cook until golden brown, moving them round the pan with a spoon so as not to burn them.

Chop the herbs and rocket finely, but not so much that they resemble tea leaves. Put them in a warm serving bowl with four tablespoons of extra virgin olive oil, a generous grinding of sea salt and black pepper, the finely chopped shallot and the lump of butter. Squeeze in the lemon juice and a couple of pinches of finely grated lemon zest.

When the pasta is cooked, drain it and add to the herbs, butter and lemon. Scatter over the warm breadcrumbs and serve.

For 2

pasta for two (any shape), about 300g

extra virgin olive oil

a large clove of garlic, crushed

2 handfuls of fresh white breadcrumbs

2 large handfuls of chopped fresh herbs as above

a handful of rocket leaves

a small shallot, finely chopped

a lump of soft butter, about the size of a walnut

juice of a lemon, plus a little grated zest

Ribbon pasta with artichokes and capers

A cool pasta dish, ideal for summer eating. Bottled artichokes vary in quality, but often the best, and sadly the most expensive, are the ones sold by the kilo in delicatessen counters.

Rinse the artichokes of their bottling oil, cut them into quarters and put them in a shallow basin. Cover them in extra virgin olive oil, add the capers, the shallot and the lemon juice. Grind over a little black pepper and set aside for half an hour, longer if you have it. Mix together the chopped anchovy fillets and chopped parsley.

   Put a large pan of water on to boil. When it boils, salt it and add the pasta. When the water returns to the boil, turn the heat down a little and cook for nine minutes or until the pasta is firm but tender. Drain the cooked pasta and toss with the anchovies and parsley and the artichokes, together with their oil. Serve warm or cool.

For 2 as a main dish
250g (about 6 medium) preserved artichokes
extra virgin olive oil
2 tablespoons capers, rinsed
a small shallot, finely chopped
the juice from half a lemon
6 anchovy fillets, rinsed and chopped
a handful of chopped parsley
ribbon pasta (pappadelle or fettuccine) for 2, about 250g

Pasta with fresh tomato sauce

Made with obscenely ripe tomatoes that have baked in the sun, this sauce is a joy, and as easy as any supper could ever be. But how often do we get tomatoes like that? Mellow, savoury balsamic vinegar seems to add sunshine to toms that miss the mark.

Pour the olive oil into a pan – deep or shallow, it makes little difference. Add the garlic and warm the oil over a medium heat. As soon as the garlic starts to fizz, add the tomatoes. They will cook down to a slush, so it matters not how small you chop them. Just don't forget to take the stalks out.

   Cook the pasta in a large pan of furiously boiling salted water for about nine minutes. Meanwhile, season the tomatoes with salt and coarsely ground black pepper and cook over a moderate heat, just spluttering and bubbling gently, for about ten minutes, until reduced to a red slush. Add a few drops of balsamic vinegar – about a tablespoon – and throw in the basil leaves. Cook for a further minute.

   Drain the pasta, but not too thoroughly (just a little of the cooking water is useful for the sauce), tip it back into the pan, then pour over the sauce. Toss quickly and eat while still fresh and lively.

For 2
olive oil, a fruity one, about a wineglassful (60ml)
2 cloves of garlic, crushed
12 ripe, medium-sized tomatoes, chopped about a bit
dried pasta for 2, any shape (about 300g)
balsamic vinegar
basil leaves, a good handful

Fragrant noodles

Noodle soup with grilled fish

For 2 as a substantial lunch or 4 as a light supper

3 tablespoons dark soy sauce

2 tablespoons sake (rice wine)

2 tablespoons mirin (sweet rice wine) or dry sherry

a clove of garlic, crushed

a teaspoon of sugar

4 fish fillets (red mullet fillets, salmon, trout, or any white fish), about 200g total weight, skinned

150g thin noodles

a little vegetable or groundnut oil

a spring onion or two, finely chopped

a lump of ginger, peeled and finely shredded

a large handful of spinach leaves

300ml ready-made stock – fish, chicken or vegetable

The type of noodle is immaterial in a soup of this sort. Anyone who tells you different just enjoys making a fuss. Chinese egg, Japanese ramen or Italian ribbon pasta, it matters little. Just use whatever is in the cupboard. Unless, of course, you are a purist. In which case you have bought the wrong book.

Mix the soy sauce, sake, mirin, garlic and sugar in a shallow dish. Put the fish steaks or fillets into the mixture and turn them to coat both sides. Leave for at least half an hour. An hour would be better.

Put a large pan of water on in which to cook the noodles. Salt it as it reaches the boil and add the noodles. Cook them for four minutes if they are Chinese or Japanese, up to nine minutes if they are Italian. Drain and put into cold water. Put a little oil in a frying pan and fry the spring onion and ginger till soft and fragrant. Add the spinach leaves, torn up a bit if large, and cook for a minute till they wilt.

Push the spinach to the side of the pan and add the fish. Cook for two minutes. Meanwhile, bring the stock to the boil. When it reaches the boil, ladle it into bowls, stir in the ginger, onion and spinach mixture and the noodles, then lay the fish on top. Eat steaming hot.

Spicy pork with noodles

For 2 as a substantial lunch or supper

250g pork (a chop would be
    ideal)
150g thin egg noodles
a litre of ready-made chicken or
    vegetable stock
groundnut oil (about 500ml)

For the marinade:

2 spring onions, finely sliced
2 tablespoons light soy sauce
a tablespoon of rice wine
a teaspoon of five-spice powder
2 large cloves of garlic, finely
    chopped
dried chilli flakes, a pinch or two
a tablespoon of lemon juice

A bowl of chicken stock with thin noodles, seasoned with lumps of spiced pork. Clear, hot and warming.

Cut the pork into strips, each about as thick as a finger. Put them in a shallow dish with the marinade ingredients. Set aside for half an hour. Longer if you have it.

Put a large pan of water on to boil, then when it is bubbling fiercely, add the noodles. Cook for four minutes, or whatever it says on the packet, then drain. Pour the water away and add the stock to the empty pan. Bring gently to the boil.

Get a wok or frying pan hot over a high flame, then pour in the oil. When the oil is hot (you can test the heat by dropping in a cube of bread and watching it turn golden), shake the pork pieces dry and drop them into the hot oil. Tip the marinade into the hot stock. Reduce the heat under the oil and cook the pork for three minutes, until golden brown and lightly crisp.

Ladle the hot stock into deep bowls, add the cooked noodles and the pork and eat straight away.

Noodles with chicken, red chilli and basil

For 2

500g chicken thighs
a tablespoon of light soy sauce
a tablespoon of rice wine or dry
    sherry
2 teaspoons cornflour
noodles for two (about 150g)
a stalk of lemon grass
groundnut oil
4 spring onions, roughly chopped
1 tablespoon Thai fish sauce
juice of a lime
3 plump garlic cloves, chopped
2 red chillies, seeded and finely
    sliced
a large handful of basil leaves

Cut the chicken from its bones, then cut it into large chunks. Bite-sized or slightly larger than bite-sized is about right. Put them in a bowl with the soy sauce, rice wine or sherry and cornflour. Set them aside for a while, about quarter of an hour should be long enough. Cook the noodles in boiling salted water till tender (about four minutes), drain and set aside.

Chop the lemon grass finely, discarding any tough layers. Heat a wok over a high heat. When it is hot, add a little oil, just enough to make a shallow puddle in the bottom. When it starts to crackle, and slightly smoke, add the chicken pieces and stir-fry them for a couple of minutes until dark golden brown. Keeping the chicken in the pan, pour off the oil.

Put the wok back on the heat and add the spring onions, fish sauce, lime juice, lemon grass, garlic, cooked noodles and chillies and continue to stir fry, moving the ingredients around the pan with chopsticks for five minutes or so, until all is sizzling and tender. Throw in the basil leaves, push them round the pan once or twice, then eat straight away.

Chicken noodle soup with coconut and lime

A long list of ingredients but the method is straightforward enough. A hot, aromatic soup, rich with coconut and tart with lemon grass and lime, substantial enough to be supper. Fish sauce and lemon grass are to be found in most of the major supermarkets and oriental stores. A lovely dish – hot and velvety.

Cut the chicken into thick slices and put it in a china, glass or stainless steel dish with the garlic, soy, fish sauce, lime juice and turmeric. Set aside for about half an hour. Very finely chop, or whiz in a blender, the lemon grass, lime zest and most of the coriander leaves. It should resemble a rough paste.

Put the chicken stock in a saucepan, add the lemon grass paste and bring to the boil. Add the noodles and cook till tender, about four minutes. Lift the noodles out of the stock, turn the stock down to a low bubble and set the noodles aside. Fry the spring onions, ginger and chillies in a little oil in a shallow pan till they sizzle and colour lightly. Add the chicken, patting it dry first, and fry till nicely golden brown. Tip all, including the marinade from the chicken, the noodles and the coconut milk, into the chicken stock and simmer for five minutes. Pour a little of the liquid into the chicken pan, and scrape up the goodness from the pan, then tip into the soup. Add the rest of the coriander leaves.

For 2 as a main dish

2 chicken breasts, boneless
2 cloves of garlic, crushed
a tablespoon of light soy sauce
a tablespoon of fish sauce (nam pla)
juice of a lime
a pinch or two of ground turmeric
2 stalks of lemon grass, roughly chopped
grated zest of a lime
a large handful of coriander leaves
500ml chicken stock
a double handful of egg noodles, about 75g
2 spring onions, thickly sliced
a lump of ginger, about as big as a walnut, peeled and grated
2 small red chillies, seeded and chopped
groundnut oil
400ml tin of coconut milk

Lentils

Beloved of Indians, Italians and hippies. Lentils – pale green, slate grey or cinnamon brown – offer an earthy, nutty note to our cooking. They require no soaking and are tender within half an hour, sometimes less. Boiled, they are boring. Stirred into softened onion and flavoured with bacon or mushrooms while they simmer, they become warm, peppery and slightly smoky. On the downside they are boringly fashionable and invariably flatulent.

Small, whole lentils are traditionally cooked till quite soft, and I think this more interesting than when they are undercooked, as is the current fad. An *al dente* lentil can be hard on the gut. Explosive even. Cooked with a generous eye on the clock, nothing else can match their texture, which is nutty and soothing at the same time. Cook them in stock, a broth made from dried mushrooms (just steep a few dried porcini in water and use that) or a mixture of water and wine. Worcestershire sauce will beef them up a bit, as will soy sauce or balsamic or sherry vinegar. A shot of lemon juice at the end of cooking will really make them sing.

Look out for the pale green Castelluccio from Italy, and the slate coloured Puy from France; their flavour is particularly earthy, peppery and deep. They keep their shape and are less likely to turn to sludge on you. Save them for the simpler recipes. Any old lentil can be used for soup.

Lentils with spinach and gravy

For 2 as a main dish
200g lentils, green or brown
spinach, a couple of handfuls
2 cupfuls of leftover gravy from
   a casserole or curry

Leftover gravy from casseroles, stews and curries is sometimes more interesting than the original dish. Quite why it sits there at the back of the fridge is anyone's guess. Get the gravy blistering hot, then use it to sauce lentils, or beans, for a casual, earthy supper.

Give the lentils a good rinse in running water, then put them on to cook, just covered with water. After twenty to twenty-five minutes check their progress. They should be really quite soft. Drain.

Wash the spinach thoroughly, then while it is still wet put into a large saucepan. Cover with a lid and put over a moderate heat for a minute or two until the leaves wilt. (They are effectively cooking in their steam.) Remove from the heat, drain and chop roughly.

In the same pan, bring the gravy to the boil. Add the cooked lentils and spinach. Check the seasoning, you may well need salt and black pepper. But of course that will depend on how your gravy was seasoned.

Lentil soup with mushrooms and lemon

The earthiness of lentils makes a rich broth that is almost meaty. Lemon, added at the end of cooking, gives a welcome smack of acidity.

Peel and roughly chop the onions. Put them in a pan with enough olive oil to cover the bottom, then cook them over a moderate heat until soft but not coloured. Add the garlic, peeled and squashed flat (just smash each clove with the flat of a knife blade), and the chilli. Cook for a minute or two, then chop the mushrooms into large juicy nuggets and stir them in.

Cover with a lid and cook for five minutes, stirring now and again. Throw in the lentils, then pour in enough stock or water to cover them twice over. Now bring the whole lot to the boil – you can add a bay leaf at this point if you have one around – then turn the heat down so that the soup is gently bubbling. Leave, with the lid almost covering the pot, until the lentils are soft. Not just tender. Soft. About thirty minutes.

Season with salt, black pepper, Worcestershire sauce (a few vigorous shakes, but the quantity is up to you) and lemon juice. The flavour should be mellow and earthy from the lentils and mushrooms, with a bite of chilli and lemon.

For 4 as a substantial lunch or supper
2 large shallots or small onions
olive oil, about 2 tablespoons
2 large cloves of garlic
1 large dried chilli
2 handfuls/100g brown mushrooms
125g/a large cupful small brown or green lentils
stock, any sort, or water, about 1 litre
Worcestershire sauce
a lemon

Buttered lentils

For 2 as a simple accompaniment to fish, chicken or game
200g/2 large handfuls of green or blue lentils
4 fat cloves of garlic, squashed flat
50g butter
balsamic vinegar
juice of a lemon

These are meant as a side dish, unless you feel up to chomping your way through an entire bowl of lentils.

Rinse the lentils in running water. Put them in a large saucepan with the garlic and cover them with water, bring them to the boil, then turn them down to a simmer. They should cook at a moderate bubble for about twenty minutes, by which time they should be tender but far from soft. Drain the lentils.

Heat the butter in a shallow pan. When it starts to froth, add the drained lentils, a good seasoning of salt, a teaspoon of balsamic vinegar to add depth, and a grinding of black pepper. Toss the lentils around in the butter. When all is hot and nutty-smelling squeeze over the lemon juice and serve.

Spiced lentils with cream and ginger

For 2
a large cupful/200g green or brown lentils
1 large shallot or medium-sized onion
2 large cloves of garlic, crushed
50g butter
a piece of ginger about the size of your thumb
2 tomatoes
1 medium-hot red chilli, seeded and chopped
100ml double cream
a teaspoon of garam masala

Cook the lentils in simmering water till tender and quite soft, about twenty minutes. Drain. Peel and slice the onion thinly, then put it into a pan with the crushed garlic and the butter. Cook slowly over a moderate heat until the onion has started to colour, turning golden and nutty brown. Grate the ginger into the buttery onions and sweat for a minute, then add the tomatoes, chopped about a bit, and the chilli. Continue cooking till all is a savoury sludge, about five minutes.

Pour in the cream and then stir in the garam masala. Cook very gently on a low heat, stirring in a little salt and black pepper at some point, for about ten minutes. Taste and adjust the seasoning if necessary, then stir in the cooked and drained lentils. When the lentils are warm, pour into a shallow dish and eat with bread or roti or as a side dish to grilled chicken or aubergines.

Beans

The cooking time of beans varies not just according to their variety but also to their age. It is impossible to tell the age of a bean just by looking at it, and few of us can remember when we bought those chick peas. The good news is that most beans are thoroughly good natured in the pot, and several minutes either way means little or nothing.

Generally I find the white beans are best for casseroles, whilst the green flageolets are better eaten with a simple olive oil dressing. Big, beautiful butter beans may need skinning – which is a real drag – so look out for split and skinned ones. Chick peas are almost impossible to overcook, and tinned ones are just as good unless you are making falafel to a traditional recipe.

White bean fritters with anchovy mayonnaise

Soak the cannellini beans overnight in deep, cold water. They will swell up to twice their size by morning.

Pour off any remaining water from the beans, cover with fresh water and put on the heat to cook at a lively simmer for forty-five minutes. By this time they will be soft but not squashy. They are done when you can squash them between your fingers. Meanwhile, mash the anchovy fillets to a paste and stir into the mayonnaise with the lemon juice and cayenne. It will keep in a screw-top jar for a few days. Indeed, probably longer.

Drain and mash the beans with a potato masher or whiz them, for a few seconds only, in the food processor. Stir in the garlic, shallot, egg and grated cheese, then season with generosity with both salt and black pepper. You can put in a bit of chilli pepper if you wish. Leave to cool. The mixture should be a stiffish paste.

Roll the mixture into rounds and flatten into little patties. Put some flour on your hands as you roll them. Otherwise you will get in a right old mess. You should get about twelve flattish patties. Drop them into the beaten egg, then the crumbs and then fry in hot, shallow oil until crisp, about three minutes on either side. Eat hot, with huge dollops of the anchovy mayonnaise and a wedge of lemon.

For 4
6 anchovy fillets, rinsed
a large cupful/200ml mayonnaise
    (home-made or from a bottle)
juice of a lemon
half a teaspoon of cayenne pepper

250g cannellini beans
2 cloves of garlic, crushed
a large shallot or small onion,
    finely chopped
an egg
75g mature farmhouse cheese
    such as Lancashire, grated
beaten egg and fine, dry
    breadcrumbs for coating
groundnut oil for frying and lemon
    to serve

Hot chick pea fritters with mint and cucumber yoghurt

Hot, garlicky Middle Eastern fritters. The mashed golden peas soak up the garlic to give a mouthful that is at first crisp, then fluffy, then hot and garlicky. They are best eaten straight from the pan, cooled by the mint-flecked yoghurt, with warm pitta bread, some sweet pickled chillies and a few ice-cold beers. A casual kitchen supper – like pretty much everything in this book.

Soak the chick peas overnight in deep, cold water with a teaspoon of bicarb. (Oh come on; it only takes about sixty seconds to empty a bag of them into a basin of cold water before you brush your teeth.) The next day drain the peas and rub them with your hands to remove most of the skins; this is both slightly messy (the skins stick to your fingers) and somehow quite pleasurable. It takes barely five minutes.

Put the chick peas in a blender or food processor – a masochist will use a pestle and mortar – with all the other ingredients except the oil and a hefty seasoning of salt (about a teaspoon). Whiz to a thick sludge. Leave to settle in the fridge for about half an hour. Meanwhile, grate the cucumber without bothering to peel it and squeeze it in your fist to wring out some of the water. Stir it into the yoghurt with a grinding of salt and the chopped mint leaves (chop them quite finely if they are the hairy sort). Chill.

Shape the chick pea mixture into balls, about twelve, and put them on a plate. Heat enough oil to come half way up a deep pan, until it is hot enough to bubble furiously when you drop your fritters in it. Fry them in two or three lots so as not to cool the oil, which would make them soggy instead of crisp. They should be ready after two minutes on each side. Lift out with a slotted spoon and drain on kitchen paper. Eat hot.

For 2

250g dried chick peas
bicarbonate of soda
3 plump, juicy cloves of garlic, crushed
an onion, chopped
a large handful of chopped coriander leaves
a teaspoon of ground cumin seeds
a teaspoon of coriander seeds, ground
a teaspoon of dried chilli flakes
half a teaspoon of baking powder
oil for deep frying

For the dipping sauce:

half a small cucumber
150ml/a large cupful of cold, thick yoghurt
a handful of mint leaves, chopped

Split pea soup with Moroccan spiced butter

For 4
300g/5 handfuls of split yellow
    peas
an onion, roughly chopped
2 large sprigs of mint
olive oil, your best

For the butter:
2 spring onions, finely chopped
2 cloves of garlic, crushed
a teaspoon of paprika
a teaspoon of ground coriander
half a teaspoon of ground chilli
a palmful of mint leaves, chopped
a small handful of coriander
    leaves, chopped
50g butter

When beans are cooked in a soup they are invariably better the following day, after they have spent time with the other ingredients. This one is worth eating the same day. A golden, deep-flavoured bowlful of beans and butter.

Soak the peas overnight in deep cold water. The next day drain, cover with fresh water and bring them to the boil. Turn the heat down and let them simmer with the onion, mint and a glug or two of olive oil.

After an hour or so they will be tender enough to crush against the side of the pan. If not, cook them for a while longer. If they are no longer covered by water, then add some boiling water to top them up. Remove all but a third of the peas and water and put it in either a blender or a food processor till smooth. Return the smooth mixture to the pot, and cook for a few minutes until it thickens.

To make the butter, which can be done at any time while the peas are cooking, mash all the ingredients together with a generous teaspoon of salt and then chill. (You probably won't need all the butter but it is difficult to make in smaller quantities. Keep it in the fridge or freezer and use on steak or chicken.)

Ladle the soup into bowls and stir a wodge of spiced butter into each one. Warm bread, of the soft, doughy, Arabic kind, is the most fitting accompaniment.

Soaking up flavour

Dark, dimly lit delis, smelling of sweet ham and salt cod, often have a shelf or two of dried beans, often in the corner by the spaghetti and the mop. All wrapped in cellophane tight enough to explode. Round ivory haricots, pale green and elegant flageolet, and white, oval cannellini – rustling in their crackling bags. There might be rose and burgundy speckled borlotti – like little candy Easter eggs; coarse, mealy kidney beans, red white and black; and smart black-eyed beans or rare palomino beans – tan and white like the horses in a western.

Across the threshold of a Middle Eastern grocer's there will be butter beans, flat and flaky. The colour of old parchment. There will be *ful medames*, brown and round, and chick peas like little beige nuggets to be whizzed into purées, rich and reeking with garlic and olive oil. A bowl of *ful medames*, warm from the pot and glistening with olive oil and lemon wedges, has been nourishment to many for thousands of years.

Split peas, both green and gold, are destined for steaming soups, while split chick peas, the *channa dhal* of India, will simmer to an ochre purée to be spiced with chilli and onion. The offering is one of warmth.

All beans have the ability to soak up the flavours with which they are cooked. The smokiness of bacon or dried mushrooms will permeate the floury fibre of a haricot bean or dried green pea; the starchy flesh of a butter bean will sponge up the aroma of the stock or sauce in the pan. This is what makes cassoulet, with its cargo of goose and fat pork, so comforting on a cold night, and why a simple dish of warm flageolets with thick, green oil and parsley is more than the sum of its parts.

Running the smooth, dry beans through the fingers gives little clue to how satisfying they will become once they have soaked up the ham stock, the goose fat, the olive oil and the spiced cream with which they are destined to share a pot. But the real point of the bean – the one thing that makes it worth eating – is its habit (be it a haricot or a cannellini) of absorbing fat. The oil, pork fat, goose fat or butter it takes in renders the bean a glorious thing.

Indian bean stew with coriander cream onions

For 4 as a substantial meal, with rice or Indian bread if you wish

250g/4 handfuls of black-eyed
   beans or haricot beans
2 onions, chopped
3 large cloves of garlic, chopped
a knob of ginger, about the size of
   your thumb, peeled and grated
a thick slice/50g butter
4 medium-sized tomatoes, halved
250ml thick yoghurt
a tablespoon of ground coriander
   seeds
2 small, medium-hot chillies
2 large handfuls of spinach, torn
   up a little

For the spiced onions:

a thick slice/50g butter
a teaspoon of cumin seeds
a medium-sized onion, thinly
   sliced
about 150ml/a small pot of double
   cream
coriander leaves, a handful,
   chopped

A fragrant, thick soup that requires little work, just patience while it cooks. The beans are good natured and will simmer undisturbed while you do other things far more interesting than cooking.

Soak the beans overnight in cold water. Drain them, put them in a deep saucepan and cover them with water. Bring to the boil, skim off the froth, then turn them down to a simmer and cook till tender. They should be quite soft in forty minutes. Pour off enough water to leave about a finger's depth above the level of the beans.

Fry the onions, garlic and ginger in the butter till soft, a few minutes, then mix all the ingredients for the beans together, except the spinach, and stir into the beans. Continue cooking, on a very low heat, for about an hour. They should barely bubble. You can stir them every now and again, and at some point you should add some salt. After an hour, mash a good half of the beans with a potato masher to give a thick savoury sludge, then stir in the shredded spinach. Continue cooking for five minutes while you make the spiced onions.

Melt the butter for the onions in a shallow pan, add the cumin seeds and onion and cook until they are golden, slightly singed on the edges. Stir in the cream and the coriander leaves. Fill bowls with the beans and spoon some of the creamed onion on top.

Tomato, bean and bacon stew

A thrown together, big bowl of bean soup, with enough fat to warm you through from head to toe. Reheated the following day it tastes even better.

Soak the beans overnight in plenty of cold water. The next day, put them on to cook, covered with fresh water, with a bay leaf or two and a glug of olive oil, and simmer until they are really quite tender. After the first few minutes' cooking you should skim off the fluffy white scum that rises to the surface. They should be ready after fifty minutes' simmering. You should be able to crush them with light pressure but they shouldn't be falling apart. Turn the heat off.

Warm a little olive oil in a large, deep pan. Enough to cover the bottom comfortably. Add the onions and the garlic and cook over a slow heat until they have softened but not browned. Throw in the bacon and the celery and cook till the fat turns golden; a couple of minutes.

Add the tomatoes and their juice, the beans, and enough of their cooking liquid to cover everything. You will probably need all of it, and even a drop of water too. You can stick the bay leaves in too. Simmer for about half an hour then add the spring greens, chopped up a bit, or shredded cabbage and the parsley leaves. There is no need to chop them. Continue cooking for about twenty minutes.

Add some salt (be generous) and black pepper. Take the pan to the table and ladle into bowls with a drizzle of olive oil and a scattering of Parmesan on each. Oh, and you'll need some bread. Leave enough for tomorrow.

For 4 as a substantial lunch or supper
250g/4 large handfuls cannellini, flageolet or haricot beans
bay leaves
olive oil, the good sort
2 medium-sized red onions, chopped
4 cloves of garlic, chopped
a couple of handfuls of diced fat smoked bacon, such as pancetta
2 sticks of celery, chopped
2 x medium-sized tins (400g) of tomatoes
4 handfuls of spring greens or shredded cabbage
parsley leaves, a handful
extra virgin olive oil
grated Parmesan cheese

Grains – the texture's the thing

Cooking with grains is pure therapy. We can take pleasure in squeezing the soaking water out of granular beige bulghur; breaking up the bobbly lumps of couscous before they go in the steamer; and running dry, golden polenta through our hands in a dreamy, brainless sort of way. Like playing with the sand on a tropical beach.

By grains I mean couscous, bulghur and the golden maize meal that is polenta. Earthy, soothing grains. Grains of comfort. I mention them not just because they are fashionable, some tiringly so, but because they fit in with the premise of this book – unpretentious, simple cooking for everyday eating. In Morocco they serve a mound of couscous with a spicy lamb stew. In London I stir wok-fried chicken, hot chilli paste, sultanas and tomatoes into the warm grain instead. Sometimes I toss in a few curry spices. The smell is friendly and reassuring. The recipe unorthodox. But who cares? It is a satisfying enough supper.

A risotto made from the dusty, pearl-white grain has a warming, nutty feel in the mouth. Chewy and smooth at the same time. A pilaf – a simple blend of rice and spice – is a good friend to the hungry. Bulghur is the nibbed, granular cracked wheat that gives crunchiness to kibbé – the Middle Eastern meatballs – and is the grain in tabbouleh, the Lebanese salad vivid with parsley and lemon. Polenta is golden stodge. Chic, golden stodge. A steaming plateful, oozing with melting mascarpone and scattered with Parmesan, is food at its most ribsticking. Fuel for a freezing night. It comes as a soft bowlful, with butter and cheese, or fried crisp like thick yellow toast – a canary-coloured croûte for stews and other spicy, juicy, sloppy things.

Rice

There is something peaceful about a bowl of cooked rice. Bland, simple and pure. Food to calm and soothe. To banish our hunger rather than dazzle us. No pyrotechnics, no loud flavours, no pizzazz.

But this is not to say rice is dull. Rice is whatever we want it to be – it can be mouth-poppingly spicy or smooth and creamy. Mood food. It will wake us up with hot-sour seasonings of chilli and lime leaves or send us to sleep with Parmesan and cream. Thai, Indian and Italian cooks give it equal prominence yet treat it very differently. To them it is a question of culture. To us, for whom rice is interesting rather than a way of life, what we do to it is more a question of fancy.

What do we want from our packet of rice? An entire meal, in which case let us go for the wet Italian risotto; a savoury accompaniment, in other words, a mildly spiced Indian-style pilaf; or is our rice to be used plain, to calm down the eye-wateringly hot seasoning of a Thai stew? It would be unkind and probably inaccurate to ask if we want it wet (risotto), moist (pilaf) or dry (boiled, fluffy rice as an accompaniment). But that is the crux of it.

Risotto

I long to say that all the talk of different rice for different uses is sheer snobbery and purist piffle. But it isn't. In practice, it is virtually impossible to make a truly creamy, satisfying and voluptuous risotto with long grain rice. It lacks the credentials that give the dish its characteristic texture. Use long grain instead of round grain rice and you will end up with a perfectly palatable plate of rice in thin stock – but it won't be risotto. And that is what you wanted for supper.

Ignore the scaremongers – making risotto is a doddle. It is only rice cooked in a bit of stock after all. The rice you need is Arborio, Vialone Nano or Carnaroli. These are special chalky, chubby, starchy varieties. Any decent supermarket will sell Arborio. Italian delicatessens will sell the other two. You might also like to try the golden, transparent rice often sold loose or in unlabelled plastic bags at the deli. Some cooks can make a suitably creamy risotto with it, though it does not quite work for me. But then . . .

Basic risotto with butter and cheese

A gentle, almost soporific supper for a cold night. Butter and grated cheese are the point of the dish so do not stint on them.

Cook the finely chopped onion in the butter in a heavy-bottomed pan. It does not really matter whether it has shallow or deep sides, despite what you may have read. Just make sure it isn't thin and dented – unless you actually like burned rice. After five minutes the onion should be pale gold and soft. Meanwhile, put the stock in another pan and bring it to a simmer. You can make the risotto with cold stock if you want to, but hot stock speeds up the process. Add the rice to the onions. Stir to coat the grains in butter and straight away add about a third of the hot stock. Turn the heat down so that the stock just bubbles gently and leave, stirring from time to time, until most of the stock has been absorbed by the rice. You will see the grains getting plumper. Add the rest of the stock and leave again, gently simmering until almost no liquid is left. Depending on the rice you are using, the total cooking time for it will be about twenty minutes, maybe less. It should have a bit of bite left in it. Tender, but still interesting in the mouth.

Turn off the heat. Add some extra butter and some grated cheese. A large knob of butter about as big as a golf ball should be more than enough but it is up to you. Or put in a little cream if you want. Stir quite vigorously for thirty seconds or so. Watch the rice become rich and creamy, but take care that you do not mash the grains to porridge. Check salt and pepper. You will almost certainly need both, even though the cheese can be a little salty. Serve immediately. Lukewarm risotto is not the same – despite what purists say.

For 2

a small onion, finely chopped
a big lump of butter, about 50g
about 900ml ready-made stock
    (chicken, vegetable or fish)
2 teacups/225g risotto rice

To finish:

butter, grated Parmesan cheese,
    cream perhaps

Pancetta and blue cheese risotto

A rich, comforting and velvety supper for a cold night. A crisp, bitter salad – chicory or frisée dressed with lemon, for instance – is a suitable accompaniment.

Gently heat the stock in a saucepan. Cook the pancetta and onion in the butter in a heavy-bottomed pan. When the onion is pale gold and soft and the fat on the pancetta golden and translucent, add the rice and stir through the butter. Add about a third of the hot stock and cook gently, as in the recipe on page 167, until the rice has absorbed almost all of the stock. Add a second third of the stock, cook slowly again, then a third. By the time the rice has absorbed most of the stock the grains should be plump and soft, yet with a little chalky bite to them. At least that is how I like them. The total cooking time for the rice will be about twenty minutes. Stir in a generous knob of butter and the blue cheese, crumbled into small lumps. Taste and season with salt and black pepper. Serve as the cheese starts to melt.

For 2

about 900ml ready-made stock
    (chicken or vegetable)
100g pancetta or bacon, diced
a small onion, finely chopped
a big lump of butter, about 50g
2 teacups/225g risotto rice

To finish:

butter, a walnut-sized lump
blue cheese such as Gorgonzola
    (although any strongly
    flavoured, creamy blue cheese
    will do), as much as you like,
    but probably about 225g

Pilaf

A pilaf is more pleasing to the nose than a risotto, but it lacks the risotto's comforting texture. A pilaf is drier, though not by any means dry. Warm and spicily fragrant with cardamom, coriander, bay and possibly saffron, a pilaf may also be home to dried fruits – raisins or apricots, for instance – and nuts such as almonds or cashews. The rules are not so hard and fast. Not that rules matter anyway. Especially when you are hungry.

A pilaf must be fragrant or it loses all point. The scent should not overpower but simply make you hungry. This means using Basmati rice, a long grain variety available from all but the most mundane of grocer's. The spices, whichever you choose, should be cooked gently in butter before the rice is added. The heat will release their fragrant oils and their flavour will gently permeate the whole dish. Cluttering the dish with everything in your spice rack will come to nothing. Two or three spices are quite enough.

Unlike a risotto, the grains of rice in a pilaf should be quite separate if it is to be good to eat. There are traditionally two keys to achieving this: first is to rinse the rice thoroughly in running cold water before cooking, to remove the starch that sticks the grains together, and the second is to leave the cooked rice to rest for five minutes before eating. But I can assure you that overcooking is much more likely to be the culprit that makes your rice sticky. I gave up giving rice anything more than a cursory rinse years ago.

A simple, fragrant pilaf

Sweet and mildly spiced. The Middle Eastern way. The ultimate accompaniment to spiced meat stews, especially those with cream or yoghurt in them.

Cook the chopped onion in the butter till soft and golden. You can use any old pan for this, as long as it has a tight-fitting lid to it. When the onion is soft, after about five minutes' cooking, add the spices and bay leaves. The cardamom pods will puff up. You are not going to eat them; their presence will flavour and aromatise the rice but you should fish them out on the plate.

When the spices are fragrant, a matter of a minute or two over a moderate heat, add the rice. Stir to coat with the butter, then pour in enough stock or water to cover the grains by 2.5cm or so. This will be about 300ml. In volume it will be slightly more than the rice. Bring to the boil, then cover with a tight-fitting lid and turn the heat down.

Leave the rice to cook for fifteen minutes. There should be puffs of steam escaping from the lid but the heat should not be high enough to make it rattle. Unless you have a very thin lid. The kitchen will be filled with a homely, comforting, slightly spicy smell. Turn off the heat but do not lift the lid. Leave for five minutes. Now you can lift the lid. Inhale. The scent will be warm and nutty, but in reality better than it tastes. So add some salt and, if you are eating this as a frugal supper for one, then a knob of butter would not go amiss.

Enough for 2 as an accompaniment to a hearty stew
a medium-sized onion, finely chopped
butter, about 50g
6 cardamom pods
a cinnamon stick
2 bay leaves (these really do seem to make a difference)
a generous large cupful/225g Basmati rice
about 300ml ready-made chicken or vegetable stock, or water

Some ways to turn a basic pilaf into supper

Basic pilaf made, it can be the backbone of any number of simple suppers. Recipes are not necessary – just use your judgement with whatever you have to hand. Sautéed chicken pieces, fried onions, chicken livers, chunks of pancetta, or even small, juicy hunks from last Sunday's roast can be added. Cook them in a little frothing butter till golden at the edges, then stir into the cooked rice. Nothing could be simpler. Appropriate seasonings such as toasted almond flakes, scissored pieces of dried apricot, figs or dates, and shelled pistachios, sliced fresh peaches or mangoes, are all possibilities. The key to a successful marriage of ingredients is to keep to one or two rather than using the pilaf as a way to get rid of all the little bits in the fridge. Tart dried fruits such as cranberries make a dazzling addition. Resist the temptation to add curry or spice pastes to the rice or you will lose the pilaf's feeling of simplicity and gentle well being.

Plain, fluffy white rice

Enough for 2

a large cupful/200g white
  Basmati or Thai fragrant rice
  (if you are using Thai rice then
  expect a somewhat sticker
  result)

Sometimes, nothing quite fits the bill like a bowl of fluffy white rice. It may be that you want it to accompany a fierce Thai or Indian stew, or perhaps it is just something bland and starchy that appeals you. In which case you are probably either after an antidote to a spate of rich meals or you are coming back from the brink. Regardless of measurements, you should use just enough water to cover the rice by about 2.5cm.

Tip the rice into a saucepan to which you can find a tight-fitting lid. Cover the rice by about 2.5cm with water. You will find that the quantity of water just about equals that of the rice. You could measure them in the same glass jug if you like. Add a little salt, a good few pinches. Cover the pan. Bring to the boil and cook at a fierce boil for thirty seconds or so, then turn down the heat. Simmer the rice for ten minutes. There should be a steady stream of steam pushing its way from under the lid. Without lifting the lid, turn off the heat and leave the rice for at least five minutes (any longer and you will have to put it somewhere warm).

When you lift the lid, stir the rice with a fork. It should be dry and quite fluffy.

Couscous

Baked couscous with chicken and spices

A warm, homely, fragrant, buttery, mildy spiced supper.

Put the couscous in a shallow ovenproof dish and cover with an equal amount of water. The liquid should just soak the grain, not flood it. Leave for fifteen minutes. Longer will not hurt.

Put the chicken pieces in an ovenproof dish. Mix the chilli, cinnamon, oil, garlic and curry powder to a paste (about 2 teaspoons of curry powder should be enough but add it to suit your taste) with a little salt and toss with the chicken pieces. Leave for twenty minutes.

Get the oven hot, 200°C/400°F/Gas 6. Put the chicken in the oven and bake for twenty minutes. Five minutes after the chicken goes in, put the couscous in, having folded in the sultanas and dotted it with butter (a thick slice/about 30g should be enough). Cover with foil.

When the chicken is fragrant and lightly browned stir it, and any bits from the dish, into the couscous, forking up the grain as you go. Dot with more butter, about the same again, and return to the oven for five minutes. Scatter over the chopped mint.

For 2 as a main dish

4 heaped handfuls/125g couscous
350g chicken, cut into large pieces, about 5cm
a teaspoon of crushed dried chilli
ground cinnamon – a couple of good big pinches
2 tablespoons olive oil
4 garlic cloves, finely crushed
curry powder
sultanas or raisins, a handful
butter
mint leaves, about a palmful, chopped

Baked couscous with summer vegetables

For 2 as a main dish

6 medium-sized tomatoes, halved

a small aubergine, cut into thin
slices

2 small/1 large red pepper,
halved and thinly sliced

3 large cloves of garlic, crushed

a large onion, thinly sliced

olive oil

250g couscous

a thick slice of butter

400g tin of tomatoes

at least a teaspoon of harissa
paste

a handful of chopped coriander
leaves

Couscous is traditionally steamed in a basket over a stew. I find this messy; some of the grains always escape and all too often the result is soggy rather than moist. Baking the grain instead, in a covered dish, simplifies the whole thing. The vegetables here are roasted, which intensifies their flavour.

Lay the vegetables, halved, sliced or crushed where appropriate, on a baking tray. Pour a generous amount of olive oil over them and toss them gently around until they are all coated. Sprinkle the vegetables with salt and roast them in a hot oven, 200°C/400°F/Gas 6, for about three-quarters of an hour, stirring them once. When they are golden brown at the edges and tender remove from the oven.

Sprinkle the couscous with water, just enough to come level with the top of the grain, then leave to swell for five minutes. Dot with butter, season with salt and black pepper, then cover with foil and bake for twenty minutes. Meanwhile, stir the tinned tomatoes into the roasted vegetables, smashing the tomatoes up a bit as you do so. Season with black pepper and the harissa sauce. Return to the oven. Serve, folded through with the coriander, with the couscous when ready.

Polenta

Soft polenta

Bring a litre and a half of water to the boil in a large saucepan. Add a heaped teaspoon of salt. You will have to measure both the water and the polenta – quantities need to be pretty accurate here. Pour the polenta into a jug to make it easier to add to the water in a steady stream. With a large whisk in one hand, jug of polenta in the other, add the grain to the boiling water, whisking constantly so that lumps do not form.

Little eruptions will appear as the mixture thickens, sending lumps of polenta blipping into the air. Beware hot polenta – it scalds. Turn the heat low so that it just bubbles occasionally. Without actually standing guard, whisk the sleepy sludge regularly so that it does not stick to the bottom of the pan.

After about thirty minutes the mush will start to come away from the side of the pan. This means it is ready. Beat in a thick slice of butter, about 50g. The mixture must be hot and sloppy. I think it should also be somewhat on the salty side.

Scoop into warm bowls while still molten and stir in more butter and generous amounts of grated Parmesan cheese. If polenta is to be good to eat it cannot have enough butter and cheese.

For 3
225g coarse yellow polenta – not the instant variety
butter, a generous 50g, plus more for the table
grated Parmesan cheese

Soft polenta with melted Gorgonzola

When the polenta is ready, stir in half the Gorgonzola and all of the butter. It will melt and ooze. Stir in the shredded basil. Bring the pot to the table and let everyone help themselves, scooping as much of the hot, soft polenta into their warm bowls as they wish, and stirring in chunks of the remaining Gorgonzola and handfuls of grated Parmesan.

For 3 as a main dish
the recipe above
about 300g ripe, creamy Gorgonzola
butter, a generous 50g
a handful of basil leaves, shredded
grated Parmesan cheese

Polenta as a side dish

Enough for 4
100g coarse yellow polenta – not
  the instant variety
butter, about 50g
double cream, at least 100ml
Parmesan cheese, grated

Like mashed potato, polenta is especially good when it meets the gravy of a casserole. Savoury brown sauce meets creamy yellow stodge. It will keep warm in the pot, covered with a butter wrapper, while you get the rest of your act together.

Bring 750ml water to the boil. Use a heavy-based saucepan so that the polenta does not burn. Add a level teaspoon of salt, then pour in the polenta in a steady stream while whisking with the other hand. As the mixture starts to thicken, take care to avoid the splutters of hot polenta that erupt. Turn down the heat and leave to cook, at a gentle pace, just the occasional blip breaking the surface, for half an hour. Stir it from time to time.

When it is ready, the mixture will come away from the side of the pan. The colour will be an incandescent yellow, the texture like creamy porridge. Stir in the butter and cream and as much grated Parmesan cheese as you wish. A little black pepper might be in order too. It is up to you. Serve the polenta in heaps on the side.

Toasted polenta

For 6 at least
the soft polenta recipe on page
  175
a little olive oil
melted butter

Toasted polenta, crisp outside, creamy and moist within, makes a good accompaniment to virtually any casserole. The set polenta will keep in the fridge for a day or two. Toast it and eat with baked beans.

Make the polenta. Cook until it is really thick, perhaps an extra five or ten minutes, and comes away from the side of the pot when you stir it. Beat in a generous amount of butter. Pour the polenta out on to a board that has been lightly oiled to stop it sticking. Pat it into a neat pile rather than a sprawling mass and leave to set.

After an hour or so it will be firm but wobbly. You can leave it like this for a day if you need to – it will come to no harm. Cover it with clingfilm and leave it somewhere cool. Cut wide slices, as thick as old-fashioned fireside toast, off the cake and brush them with a little oil or melted butter. Put the slices on a hot griddle pan sitting over the hob, or in a frying pan with a light coating of olive oil or butter. Cook until the polenta is crisp on both sides, turning once. Brush with melted butter and season.

Bulghur

Bulghur – cracked wheat grain – is not the rarity it was. Any decent supermarket worthy of its name will have cellophane bags of the beige, nibbed grain. It is not big on flavour. The point of bulghur – however you care to spell it – is its texture and smell. Warm and nutty. It must be soaked before use, a matter of ten minutes, and can be thrown straight into a salad (with parsley, tomatoes and mint) or mixed with ground lamb or chopped mushrooms to make a substantial main dish.

Mushroom and pine nut kibbé

Cook the chopped onions in enough oil to cover the bottom of a medium-sized shallow pan. While they soften over a moderate to low heat, soak the bulghur in enough cold water to cover it. Stir the cinnamon and garlic into the onions and continue cooking till all is soft, pale gold in colour and fragrant.

Cut the mushrooms up a little; in halves or quarters depending on their size. They should be a bit bigger than bite-size. Tip half of the cooked onions into the bulghur and return the rest to the stove. Add a little more oil and, when it is hot, the mushrooms. Cover with a lid and cook for about six or seven minutes, or until the mushrooms are tender and juicy. Season with salt and black pepper. Toss in the pine nuts, mint and the chopped tomatoes and cook for a further ten minutes. Remove the lid and continue cooking for a couple of minutes till the liquid has almost all evaporated; but don't let the mixture dry.

Generously butter a shallow baking dish, the size of a small roasting tin. Pile half of the onion bulghur in the tin and pat it down a little. Tip the mushroom filling on top, then the rest of the onion bulghur. Dot generously with butter. You can throw over a few pine nuts if there are any left. Bake in a preheated oven (180°C/350°F/Gas 4) for twenty minutes until golden and singing. Meanwhile, mix the yoghurt and mint and chill. Serve in big dollops with the hot kibbé.

For 4

4 medium-sized onions, chopped
olive oil
4 handfuls (200g) of bulghur
a teaspoon of ground cinnamon
2 plump cloves of garlic, chopped
4 handfuls (400g) of mushrooms
a handful of pine nuts
a handful of chopped mint
2 medium-sized tomatoes,
    chopped
butter

To serve:

200g thick natural yoghurt and a
    handful of chopped mint
    leaves

Tabbouleh

For 4 as a main-course salad

a handful of bulghur wheat

a large bunch of bright and bushy
parsley

a large bunch (about 50g) mint

2 or 3 large spring onions

4 medium-sized tomatoes, ripe
and juicy

the juice of a large lemon (at
least 2 tablespoons)

4 tablespoons green, fruity olive
oil

Misplaced, misspelled and misunderstood. Tabbouleh is a Lebanese salad that should dazzle the mouth with lush amounts of bushy, ultra-fresh parsley and lemon juice. Too often, though, the grain exceeds the green, turning the refreshing into the dull and chewy. As a side dish, this simple salad excels with both meat and fish (it is unbeatable on the same forkful as a piece of plain pan-fried plaice) but try it too with goat's cheese, ham carved off the bone or thick slices of smoked salmon. I remain unconvinced that this is a job for the food processor – even the best cannot compete with proper knife-chopped parsley. So get the knife-sharpener out. (What did you expect from a book called *Real Cooking?*)

Rinse the wheat in a sieve under cold running water, then soak it in enough water to cover for ten minutes. Squeeze dry with your fist, then tip into a salad bowl. Cut the stalks off the herbs and get chopping. Both parsley and mint leaves should be chopped finely, but not so finely that they look like tea leaves and their flavour ends up soaking into the chopping board. Scrape the chopped leaves into the wheat, then cut the spring onions – both the white and the best of the green bits – into small pieces.

Cut the tomatoes into small dice, losing as little of their juice and jelly as possible. Add them to the salad with the spring onions, lemon juice, olive oil and a generous seasoning of salt and pepper. Toss together. Leave for a few minutes – fifteen will do – for the flavours to marry, then eat as a side dish or as a principal dish by scooping the salad up in crisp iceberg lettuce leaves. Perfect picnic fodder, though a night in the fridge will do it no favours at all.

Vegetables

Vegetables deserve pride of place at the table. An oval platter of asparagus perhaps, bought cheaply at the market, then roasted and buttered; a dish of golden baked onions oozing with melted cheese; a roasted aubergine hissing with olive oil and spices. Only the unremittant carnivore would insist on his lump of flesh to accompany such vegetable delights.

We long ago stopped eating vegetables just because they were good for us. We now see them, or perhaps I should say most of us see them, as capable of standing alone as the point of a meal. I cannot be alone in regarding a baked potato, its skin crisp and salty, its flesh fluffed and buttery, as being a perfectly decent supper as it is. Though a few gherkins and a slice from a big cheese on the side wouldn't go amiss.

While a dish of green beans, served hot and slightly limp as an accompaniment to a piece of fish, can be a perfect thing, more substantial dishes can be regarded as supper: a gratin of chicory wallowing in a mustardy cheese sauce, those aubergines again, this time grilled with Parmesan cheese, or a pile of crisp and melting potato cakes. If I have added a bit of bacon to them its point is as a seasoning rather than a condescension to the carnivore. Vegetarians can just leave it out.

The best vegetables are those that have been grown locally and arrive on your doorstep as soon as possible after harvest.

Just think of freshly cut lettuce, its milky white sap still dribbling from its stem. This is not to put down the crisp green beans flown from Kenya, the darling little potatoes from Jersey or the Italian tomatoes sold on the vine, but it is to say that if we get a choice, then we may find that locally grown tastes better. Freshness counts. That is, of course, if we get a choice.

While the big supermarkets offer us shelves of brilliant greens, neatly trimmed and ready for the pot, not to mention an impressive display of unusual or out-of-season produce from farther shores, it is the 'organic box scheme' that seems set to change the face of our vegetable buying. Brought right to our door, the box scheme can supply us with pure, chemical-free vegetables (and indeed fruit) at a fair price. All they ask is that we take pot luck on what is available. Some will offer its regulars a choice, but most people I know are happy with the surprise element.

You may find some surprises in this chapter. A way of cooking carrots, for instance, that roasts them with butter and bacon, or one for simmering courgettes slowly in olive oil and herbs. Fennel is pan-fried with Parmesan cheese and tomatoes are roasted before they appear in a salad. I believe that vegetables respond better to such bold, unfussy treatment rather than ending their days puréed, piped and pointless.

The green salad

A daily ritual of leaves, torn and tossed. I would have made a good rabbit. My appetite for greens is unquenchable. I have them on my kitchen table on a daily basis. Nothing fancy – usually raw in a plain white bowl, tossed with a thick and mustardy dressing.

Some people come over all extravagant about making a green salad. This is not always a good thing. The most interesting ones to eat are often those that have been heavily edited. I just throw a handful of leaves, rarely more than two sorts, into a bowl and dress it with something slippery, such as olive oil, melted cheese, seasoned cream or yoghurt. There should be tartness in there somewhere – either in the leaves, perhaps rocket or chicory, or in the dressing, say mustard or wine vinegar.

In high summer, the salad can be the whole meal – though at that point it is usually stuffed with salty feta cheese, scarlet tomatoes, French beans and basil. Or spinach leaves, crisp bacon and a creamy dressing. But a plateful of tiny crisp leaves, sharp with lemon juice and fruity olive oil, often fits the bill.

Lettuces bolt from every greengrocer's shop and supermarket stand. Crunchy, long, lush Cos; frilly, silly, pointless lollo rosso. There are jolly, round butterheads with silky leaves tender as a petal. So lovely in a white bread sandwich for tea. Hard, round iceberg will crunch but deliver little flavour. Though it will tame a few racy rocket or watercress leaves. Just don't overdo it.

As a sponge for cleaning the sauce from a plate, a green salad cannot be beaten. The leaves soften in the hot gravy, melting into it. Try following liver and fried onions with a salad of baby spinach leaves, or use floppy butterhead lettuce leaves to mop up the gravy from roast pork.

Lettuce and olive oil

crisp Cos lettuce
extra virgin olive oil, something
    fruity
a lemon

Separate the leaves and wash them under running water. Tear them into manageable lengths, but don't overdo it. Shake them dry and put them in a bowl. Mix a little olive oil with some salt, freshly ground pepper and a generous squeeze of lemon juice. Taste and add more salt, or pepper or lemon, until you have a simple dressing that is to your taste. I suggest you may like to start with about four times as much oil as lemon juice. Pour the dressing over the torn leaves and toss gently with a spoon. Use as an accompaniment for absolutely anything. Especially roasts instead of veg.

Watercress and walnut oil

a bushy bunch of watercress
walnut oil
lemon juice
a few leaves of mild lettuce such
    as Cos or Little Gem

Cut the roots off the watercress and rinse it thoroughly. Shake it dry enough for the leaves to separate rather than stick together.

Mix a little walnut oil – a couple of tablespoons is enough – with some salt. There is pepper enough in the watercress. Soften the roast-nuttiness of the oil with a few squeezes of lemon juice. Toss the lettuce, torn about a bit, and the watercress, with the dressing. Eat straight away, before the dressing has time to turn the watercress black and floppy.

Rocket salad

For 2 as a side dish
rocket leaves, a few handfuls
3 tablespoons extra virgin olive oil
    (a fruity one)
juice of half a lemon

Rocket has a pungent pepperiness that is welcome in the sea of mild-mannered salad leaves at the supermarket. Served with a steak or grilled chop, it is an unbeatable mop with which to clean your plate – rocket leaves and meat juices being a marriage made in heaven.

Rinse the rocket and shake it dry. Mix the oil and lemon and season generously with salt. Toss the leaves in the dressing and eat before they wilt.

Rocket and Parmesan

Wow. A gutsy little plateful, peppery with rocket and salty with Parmesan.

Wash and shake dry the rocket leaves. Put them on a large plate. Shave off slices of Parmesan cheese with a vegetable peeler or sharp knife. You probably will not need all the cheese but it is easier to shave from a large piece. The slices should be thin enough to see through. Lay them on top of the rocket. Mix the olive oil with the wine vinegar, adding salt as necessary. Shake in a few dashes of balsamic vinegar, which will mellow the whole thing a little. Add as much as you like, tasting as you go; I suggest about a teaspoonful. Pour the dressing over the salad.

For 1

rocket leaves, a couple of
    generous handfuls
about 100g Parmesan cheese, in
    the piece
extra virgin olive oil, about 3
    tablespoons
red wine vinegar, a couple of
    tablespoons
balsamic vinegar, a few dashes

Red leaf, raw mushroom and Gruyère

For 2 as a light lunch or supper
2 thick slices of bread
groundnut oil, a little
a clove of garlic
a head each of radicchio and oak
    leaf lettuce
2 handfuls/about 300g coarsely
    grated Gruyère cheese
a shallot, very finely chopped
a handful of parsley, chopped
2 handfuls of mushrooms, sliced

For the dressing:
2 tablespoons Dijon mustard
a tablespoon of red wine vinegar
half a wineglass of mild olive oil

A great mixture of textures. A meal in itself. The bread cubes make the salad, so to miss them out is to short-change yourself.

Cut the bread into cubes. The size is up to you but none should be so large that you cannot get anything else on your fork. Leaves and croûtons are a good combination. Fry the bread in a little oil with the whole peeled garlic until golden. Sprinkle with salt and drain on kitchen paper.

Wash the leaves and tear them up into manageable pieces. They should not be too small, as soft lettuces such as oak leaf go soggy if they are not eaten straight away. Put them in a salad bowl with the grated cheese, chopped shallot and parsley and the slices of raw mushroom.

Mix the mustard and the vinegar, then whisk in the olive oil slowly, using a fork or a small whisk. It should thicken slightly. Stir in a little salt and pepper. Pour the dressing over the salad and toss gently, taking care not to smash the delicate leaves. Throw the fried bread over the salad. A gloriously munchy, savoury plateful.

Vinaigrette – a punchy dressing for a salad

Enough for a salad for 4
2 tablespoons red wine vinegar
a heaped tablespoon of Dijon
    mustard
salt
black pepper, freshly ground
5 tablespoons olive oil

Mopping up the savoury cooking juices on your plate with a handful of salad leaves is the best dressing a salad can get. But then the rest of the salad needs interesting lubrication too. I always try to include chopped parsley in my green salads, sometimes adding it to the vinaigrette. The quality of the oil and the vinegar is pretty much the crux of it. Nut oils, such as walnut or hazelnut, are flattering to the leaves, but are often better if used with a little olive oil to dampen down their ardour. I like my vinegars with a bit of a bite to them, but not so much that they make your eyes water.

Put the vinegar and mustard in a small jar, one to which you have a lid. Grind in about a quarter teaspoon of salt and several grinds of pepper. Pour in the olive oil, then screw on the lid and shake vigorously until you have a thick, limpid dressing. Taste, adding more mustard, vinegar and seasoning as you think fit. The dressing will keep in the fridge for several days, probably longer. I don't know because I use it almost daily.

Frisée and bacon

For 2 as a light lunch dish or first course

200g bacon in the piece, or
  pancetta
2 thick slices of good bread
2 tablespoons Dijon mustard
2 tablespoons red wine vinegar
100ml (a wineglass) groundnut or
  light olive oil
4 generous handfuls of frisée
  (curly endive)

Probably the best salad in the world. Probably.

Cut the bacon into dice, roughly the same size as dolly mixtures. Don't tell me you don't know how big dolly mixtures are. Cut the bread into slightly larger dice, a couple of centimetres square. Whisk the mustard, vinegar and most of the oil with a little salt and pepper until thick. Set aside.

In a frying pan, cook the bacon dice in a little oil. Just enough to stop them sticking to the pan. When the fat starts to turn golden, add the cubes of bread.

Rinse the frisée in cold water, using only the whitest, crispest, curliest bits. Shake dry and put in a bowl. Toss the bacon and bread around in the pan from time to time. When the bacon is golden brown and sizzling, pour it and any juices from the pan over the frisée. Tip the dressing over and toss the salad and bacon gently, coating all the leaves. Eat straight away, while the bacon is still warm.

Chicory

Underrated and underused. Chicory's trump card is its bitterness but this is also probably the reason for its lack of popularity. We like our vegetables sweet don't we? Witness the absurd success of mange-tout and those horrid little mini-sweetcorns. Candy-bar vegetables.

There is a pure, almost virginal quality to chicory as it lies in its box of deep-blue waxed paper at the greengrocer's. The blue paper is there to keep the light out, which would turn the leaves green. A tender vegetable, shaped like a magnolia about to flower, creamy-white with ruffles of palest green at the lips of its crisp leaves. Its bitter crunch is a welcome addition to a salad of sweeter leaves.

Season it boldly. Smoked bacon, mustard, blue cheese and salty black beans, flatter rather than smother chicory's flavour. When it is turned slowly in butter, some of its bitter shudder gives way to melting sweetness, the tips of its leaves caramelising in the heat. A tantalising plateful. It will take the smack of wine and lemon juice or the suavity of cream. Slit in half and left unattended in a pan with butter and a modicum of water, it will cook to tenderness and produce a delicious juice which should not be wasted.

A bulb of chicory, seasoned with grain mustard and wrapped in bacon, is the only reason I know for going to the bother of making a cheese sauce. Though I have to say that simply pouring cream and Parmesan over the naked bulbs and leaving them in the oven for half an hour is almost as good.

Blue cheese and chicory salad

Creamy, crunchy, salty and piquant. A blue with a salty bite to it, rather than a mild creamy one, will be more of a match for the bitterness of the leaves. In other words, Roquefort rather than Gorgonzola.

Separate the chicory leaves and put them in a china or glass bowl. Crumble the cheese into small lumps and drop them into the leaves. Break the walnuts up, or chop them roughly and add them too.

Whisk the oil, mustard and lemon juice with a little freshly ground black pepper. No salt. Stir in the cream. Toss with the salad ingredients and serve straight away.

For 2 as a substantial salad
2 plump and perfect heads of white chicory
200g blue cheese, preferably, but not necessarily, Roquefort
a handful of walnuts

For the dressing:
3 tablespoons mild oil (light olive, groundnut etc.)
3 tablespoons Dijon mustard
2 tablespoons lemon juice
small pot of double cream

Bacon and chicory gratin

For 2 as a main dish, 4 as a side order

3 large heads of chicory
a walnut-sized lump of butter
a little lemon juice
12 rashers of good smoked bacon
Dijon mustard
grated Gruyère cheese, a big
   handful/150g
a large pot/about 300ml double
   cream

The classical way of preparing a gratin is to infuse milk with onion, peppercorns and bay leaves and to make a roux – the mixture of flour and butter that forms the basis of a white sauce. The milk is then whisked in and left to cook gently for anything up to half an hour. It is an essential part of the repertoire of classical French sauces. Sod that for a lark. This is a deeply savoury dish, and rich enough to kill. Eat with crisp frisée or plain boiled potatoes.

Remove any brown-edged leaves from the chicory, halve the chicory and chisel out the thick stem. Melt the butter in a shallow pan, add the chicory and squeeze in a little lemon juice to stop it browning. Cook over a low heat until tender, about ten to fifteen minutes, turning from time to time.

Remove the chicory from the pan, cool a little and wrap each piece in a couple of slices of bacon. Put the heads into an ovenproof dish and pour over any juices that there may be in the pan (there may not be any at all). Stir a couple of good heaped tablespoons of mustard, more if you wish, and a handful of Gruyère into the cream, together with a good grinding of black pepper. Pour the seasoned cream over the bacon-wrapped chicory.

Bake in a moderate oven (190°C/375°F/Gas 5) for thirty minutes, turning up the heat for the last ten minutes or so to brown.

Fennel

The aniseed crunch of a fat white bulb of fennel makes it one of the most striking of all our vegetables. It has neither the earthiness of cabbage nor the sweetness of peas. Crisp, white and clean, fennel is a one-off. Buy bulbs that are smooth, white and hard as rock. They discolour and soften as they age. What it shares with most other vegetables is a hatred of water. Boiled fennel does not grab the attention. Fried in butter, stewed in cream or baked slowly in stock, it shows off its aniseed bite. A few slices tossed with lemon juice, olive oil and some crumbled goat's cheese is one of the cleanest-tasting lunches imaginable.

Slow pan-fried fennel

A flattering accompaniment to a grilled or pan-fried plaice. A gentle, peaceful sort of meal.

Cut the fennel in half from stalk to root, then again into quarters. Melt enough butter in a shallow pan to give a deep pool, about 75g, then add the fennel. Fry for a minute or two over moderate heat, then turn. Pour in enough water to come half-way up the fennel. Squeeze in the lemon juice, and throw in a little salt. Bring to the boil, then cover with a lid and cook over a low heat until the fennel is tender, about twenty minutes.

   Remove the lid and turn up the heat. The buttery cooking liquid will now start to evaporate. When only a few tablespoons of liquid are left (shake the pan from time to time), scatter over a handful of grated Parmesan. Put the lid back on for a minute or two, no longer, then eat as the cheese starts to melt, not forgetting to spoon over the remaining concentrated pan juices.

For 2 as a side dish, perhaps for fish or pork
2 large bulbs of fennel, white and hard
butter
a lemon
grated Parmesan cheese

Fennel, watercress and orange salad

For 2 as an accompaniment to plainly cooked fish, or as a light lunch with bread and cheese

a fat, hard bulb of fennel

2 bunches of watercress

a large, juicy orange

4 tablespoons thick natural
   yoghurt

olive oil

Slice the fennel bulb in half, then into thin slices; they need not be paper thin. Rinse in cold running water, then shake dry. Cut the roots and toughest stalks off the watercress having first run the bunches under the cold tap. Put into a bowl with the fennel. Peel the orange, then cut it in half from stalk to navel. Slice the orange halves across the segments to give semi-circles of orange flesh. Add to the fennel.

Mix the yoghurt with salt, black pepper and a little olive oil, about a tablespoon, whisking with a fork. Tip it over the salad and toss gently. Serve soon, before the watercress goes limp.

Baked fennel with pancetta and cream

For 2 as a main dish with green salad, or 4 as an accompaniment

4 fennel bulbs

a good handful of diced pancetta
   or bacon (about 200g)

2 cloves of garlic, finely sliced

200ml double cream

Cut each fennel bulb in half from stalk to root, then again to give four wedges. Put them in a shallow baking dish. Fry the diced bacon with the sliced garlic in a shallow pan in its own fat; if it appears dry then add a little oil or butter. When the fat and garlic are golden, tip into the fennel dish. Season with a little salt and a grinding of black pepper. Pour over the cream and bake in a hot oven, 190°C/375°F/Gas 5, until the fennel is tender to the point of a knife, about twenty-five minutes.

Asparagus

Opinions divide about the cooking of asparagus, although everyone agrees that the fresher the spears are the deeper the flavour will be. Watch your greengrocer's display carefully and buy the day it comes in, or check each bundle thoroughly, making sure the flower buds are closed tight and the ends are not too dry and cracked.

Asparagus can be boiled or steamed, grilled or roasted. It does not take well to frying. I add it to a stir fry from time to time, though it always seems out of place. I hope the salty soy will be as suitable a seasoning as cured ham, a traditional salty partner, but the soy is too bullying for such a fine and regal vegetable. The point of cooking asparagus is to make it sensuous as well as tender, and to remove the slight bitterness that can be present in the raw spear. Its flavour seems most remarkable when it is eaten warm. Rather than hot from the pot or cold from the refrigerator.

Untie the spears from their bundle. Trim away the toughest of the stalks but leave something firm to hold them by. Rinse gently in cold water, taking care not to snap them.

Cooking asparagus

The traditional method involves tying the spears together and cooking them in enough boiling, salted water to come half way up their length. The point is to boil the tougher, thicker stalks while the tips cook gently in the steam. There is a specially designed pan for such a method, which incorporates a removable, slotted inner sleeve to keep the spears upright. This is too much fuss, even for royalty.

Put a large, deep-sided pan of water on to boil. As it comes to the boil, bubbling furiously, salt it. Add the asparagus spears, either tied in a bundle with string or sitting in a wire basket smaller than the pan. This way they can be removed without damaging their tender points. Immerse them fully in the water and cover with a lid. After five minutes, pierce the lower stalks with a knife point; if it glides in then remove the asparagus. If not, return the lid and cook a little longer. The time depends on the freshness and girth. A 450g bundle is enough for two.

Tender, purple and proud

Only a prude can ignore the sexual overtones of *Asparagus officinalis*. Sitting opposite someone devouring a plate of warm
asparagus spears eaten in the traditional way – with fingers
instead of forks – my imagination has wandered more than
once. This tender vegetable is known as the king of vegetables,
as much for its flavour as its price. Its root is known as a crown.
From May till July, tied in fat bundles, the pointed stalks sit on
market stalls like coronets among the cabbages.

My cat and I often share a plate of asparagus come early
June, when the supplies of English-grown spears approach a
glut and the price falls to an affordable sum. Just the two of us
with no one to tut at such apparent decadence. Bliss for around
a pound. There is something serene about a dozen fat green
and mauve spears on a large white plate. A simple and sensuous
plateful to be eaten with respect rather than wolfed like a por-
tion of hot, salty chips.

Nothing can spoil the joy of finding the first, expensive local
asparagus in early May, no matter how much is flown in year
round from Chile and Spain. As the pace of the season quick-
ens, and spears shoot up along the rows of neatly tilled fields in

Norfolk, Suffolk and Worcestershire, the prospect of such a luxurious plateful becomes a possibility for all.

I long to taste the thin spears of climbing wild asparagus that sprout from derelict walls come spring in Southern Italy. They have both enchanted Patience Gray and evaded Elizabeth David, who found she was actually eating hop shoots. The nearest we get to such *Asparagus acutifolius* here is the fine, quivering sprue sold in the markets for a song. I am happy to sing its praises. Recommended and sold for soup, its flavour is underrated. Trimmed of its tough ends and curled round like spaghetti, it will cook in two minutes.

When prices fall dramatically as the season ends, there is still a touch of luxury about such a supper – and for less gold than the same weight of peas. By July, the English season all but spent, smooth green soups will be chilling, mild-flavoured purées may sit alongside poached salmon, and fat, steamed asparagus tips will have been stirred into creamy scrambled eggs. We will have had our fill till next year.

Asparagus with melted butter

For 2, as a starter
450g/1 bundle of English
   asparagus
75g butter

It will need a little lubrication. A light, mild olive oil will do. Any oil too fruity or peppery may overpower. Butter is better. While the spears are cooking, soften, rather than melt, some sweet unsalted butter. It must be very fresh as any taint from the fridge does not go unnoticed in such simple fare.

Cook the asparagus as on page 197. Meanwhile, soften the butter in a small pan or in a warm basin set close to the cooker. Remove from the heat when it is soft enough to dip your finger in and leave a deep hole, but catch it before it becomes transparent. Drain the asparagus. Place the spears on large plates. Whisk the butter with a fork till smooth, then pour it over the tips. Tilt the plates slightly so that the butter runs to one side. Eat the spears with your fingers, dipping the points into the golden butter. Only the coy would use a knife and fork.

Asparagus with buttered crumbs

For 2, as an indulgent starter or
light meal
450g/1 bundle of asparagus
150g butter
100g fresh white breadcrumbs

You may want a contrast to the spears' soft flesh. I have seen flaked almonds suggested for such a purpose, which is silly because they fall off as you eat. Breadcrumbs, fried in butter till golden and crisp, offer a pleasantly contrasting crunch. And they stick to the spears.

Cook the asparagus as on page 197. As soon as the asparagus hits the water, melt half the butter in a shallow pan over a low to medium heat. Add the breadcrumbs and cook until golden, turning constantly with a spoon so that they colour evenly without burning. Drain the asparagus thoroughly. It is worth a clean tea towel to make sure it is not at all wet. Place the spears on warm plates. Drop the remaining butter in the hot pan, tilt the pan from side to side to soften the butter, then pour it over the asparagus. Scatter with the toasted crumbs.

Roast asparagus

The dry, searing heat of grilling or roasting has a very different effect on asparagus from the moist methods of steaming and boiling; it brings out its bright, clear flavours. Though at the expense of sensuality, I think. Roasted asparagus has a little more bite than asparagus that has been cooked in water.

I use butter rather than olive oil for roasting asparagus. Infused with the salty tang of prosciutto and Parmesan, it makes a delectably savoury lubricant. The addition of prosciutto both provides contrast of texture and means that the dish could become a light lunch with little more than bread.

Spread an ovenproof dish with half of the butter. Roll up the prosciutto and cut it into thin strips. Scatter the strips over the buttered dish – easily done, though they will probably have stuck together. Place the asparagus in the dish and dust over the grated Parmesan. Add the rest of the butter, in small cubes.

Roast for approximately twenty minutes, at 200°C/400°F/Gas 6, basting the spears with the salty, smoky butter after ten minutes or so. Eat warm with the basting butter and crusty bread.

For 2 as a starter or 1 as a light lunch

75g unsalted butter

50g/2 thick slices of prosciutto

225g asparagus, not much thicker than a pencil

2 tablespoons grated Parmesan cheese

Greens

There are greens to suit our every mood – soft-leafed baby spinach, crunchy, hot white cabbage, tart and slithery sorrel, earthy, bullying kale, and mustard-hot gaai-choy. Plump, squat pak choy offers both tender green leaves and crisp, refreshing stems. Frilly, floppy spring greens boast robust flavour and tender spears.

Their differences are just as apparent when they are tossed in a red-hot pan with ginger, garlic and soy sauce. Where they all merge into one is when they meet a large pot of boiling water – one that reduces them all to rank, green slush. If there is one thing to take away from this chapter it is never to let greens come into contact with large quantities of hot water. Oil, yes. Water, no.

Cabbage only stinks when boiled in water. Tossed around in sizzling oil it smells fresh, green and tempting. Brussels sprouts, my *bête noire* of the vegetable world, should be kept as far from water as possible. How can anything that smells as if it has already been digested be good to eat? Though shred them with a big knife and toss them with oil, chilli and garlic and you have a vegetable to relish.

If the more bullish brassicas (Savoy cabbage, gaai-choy – Chinese mustard greens – and Brussels) are not for you, then try the gentle greens – the pak choy and the paper-thin leaves of baby spinach. Thrown into a large pan of hot oil with sizzling garlic, spring onions and chilli, then splashed with soy sauce, it is impossible to go wrong. Just ignore anyone who tells you to boil them.

Sizzling greens

Shred the greens, no more than you are able to fit comfortably in a wok or large pan. They can be sliced neatly, torn to bits or barely touched – the only important thing is that the pieces are roughly the same size, so that they cook evenly.

Peel the garlic cloves, one clove for each double handful of shredded greens, then squash them with the flat of a knife blade and your fist. Pour a little oil into a wok or large pan. It should cover the base completely but be hardly visible. Warm the oil over a moderate heat, a matter of seconds, then add the garlic cloves. When they start to sizzle and the oil is lightly shimmering, throw in the greens.

Cook for a minute or two until they have started to wilt. Kale will take a little longer than spinach. They will turn a bright, rich green. Toss them around as they cook, they will become bitter if they brown, then grind over some pepper and a little salt, by which time they will be cooked. Fish out the bits of garlic as you serve the greens, they have done their work.

robust greens – kale, cabbage,
large-leafed spinach, Brussels
garlic
olive oil

Chilli greens

Rinse the greens in cold running water. Warm some groundnut oil in a wok or large pan over a moderate heat. Shred the ginger finely; it should be like small matchsticks. Throw the sliced garlic cloves into the pan, then the ginger, the chopped spring onions and the chopped chillies. Stir fry for about thirty seconds.

Add the shredded greens, salt and a little ground black pepper. Pour in a little water, no more than a couple of tablespoons. Continue to stir fry, over a moderate heat, while all is bubbling and sizzling. If it is not, then turn the heat up. When all is hot, shake over a little sesame oil, though this is not essential, and eat immediately.

For 2
2 or 3 double handfuls of greens
(any sort, even sprouts),
shredded
groundnut oil
a knob of ginger, about as big as
a walnut, peeled
2 fat garlic cloves, thinly sliced
4 spring onions, finely chopped
3 small red chillies, seeded and
finely chopped
sesame oil

Green and pleasant

A side order of greens will flatter almost any dish in this book. There is not much that you can put on your fork that will not benefit from a partnership with something green and piquant. On a quiet evening, a heaped plate of pak choy or spinach spiced with soy sauce and garlic may make a perfectly pleasant solitary supper. Especially if it follows a few nights of excess. Greens cleanse and invigorate.

Greens are as easy to buy as they are to cook. A sniff and a squeeze will tell all. Squeeze young spring greens, their heavily veined bottle-green leaves perky with cold, to check for a firm heart underneath. Hold a bunch of purple sprouting as if it were a bunch of daffs: if it stands erect then it is fit to buy; if it flops then pass it by. The neatness of a posy of broccoli, veiled in film and secured with blue rubber, is almost irresistible. But there is more earthy flavour in the Brussels sprout tops next to it, or even the Savoy cabbage, if you are strong enough to carry the crinkly, dusky blue-green thing home.

Chinatown and oriental street markets tease us with soldierly rows of pak choy, with their white stems and green leaves the shape of soup spoons. They offer a refreshing and slightly bitter crunch. The floppy, bright green gaai-choy, hot with mustard flavours and at its best just as the little yellow flower buds open, is often there too. Much more fun than sprouts.

At the market, buy what is perky and lush. The leaves should squeak as you rummage through the box. Avoid anything that looks as if it has done a day's work. A few holes in the outside leaves are probably a good sign. Slugs seem to have an eye for the best. At the supermarket, where the greens have been bagged, we must peer through the plastic as best we can, leaving behind anything that looks yellow or sad. Greens of any sort should be bushy and proud. They should be in fine fettle.

An earthy spiciness is present in all but the most tender young greens – and those belong anyway in the salad bowl. There is bitterness, too, if you want – Brussels sprouts, frilly, coarse-leafed kale and gaai-choy have it aplenty, making a plate of hot, silky greens with rich, sweet oyster sauce such a delectable thing.

Cabbage, sprouts, kale, spinach, sprout tops, purple sprouting, spring greens – all look good on a simple white oval plate, their lush, deep-green leaves alive with Eastern spice or Western butter. Oh, and I almost forgot – they are very, very good for us. But of course, that is another matter.

Soy greens

For 1, as an accompaniment

greens, 2 double handfuls (about 200g)

groundnut or vegetable oil

garlic, a couple of large cloves

soy sauce

Again, any thick-stemmed greens, purple sprouting, spring greens or cabbage are suitable for the hot and soy sauce treatment. Serve with the roast shallots on page 226 for a succulent vegetable supper.

Tear the leaves up, or shred them with a large knife into manageable pieces. Wash them under cold running water. Heat a couple of table-spoons of oil in a wok or large pan, just enough to cover the bottom of the pan. When it is hot and slightly shimmering, squash the garlic cloves, then add them to the oil. Their job is to scent the oil – nothing more.

When the oil is crackling and bubbling around the garlic, toss in the greens. There will be an almighty spit and crackle. The smell of garlic will rise up. Cook them for about four minutes, moving them round with chopsticks (it makes not the slightest bit of difference what you use but chopsticks will make you feel the part), until they have wilted and their colour is bright. Add a few shakes of soy sauce. Six will do. The amount is up to you but the coarser-tasting greens will actually take quite a bit of it – soy seems to mellow their bitter earth-iness.

Serve hot, blisteringly hot, salty and green from the pan.

Stir-fried greens with mushrooms and oyster sauce

For 2 as a side dish, 1 as a main dish
about 250g of greens, kale,
     broccoli or cabbage
4 large handfuls (about 150g) of
     mushrooms
groundnut oil
2 cloves of garlic, chopped
rice wine or dry sherry
dark soy sauce
oyster sauce

Oyster sauce is available from most of the major supermarkets – in the oriental food section.

Shred or cut the greens into manageable pieces, remembering that broccoli is not the easiest vegetable to lift with chopsticks. Cut the mushrooms in half, unless they are quite large, when quarters would be more appropriate.

Heat a little oil in a wok or large pan. The amount you need depends on the size of your pan. There should be just enough to make a shallow puddle in the bottom. When the oil is really hot, almost smoking, add the garlic, move it quickly round the pan, then add the greens and the mushrooms. Stir them as they fry, moving them round in the hot oil for three or four minutes, until the mushrooms are golden and the greens are tender. Try not to burn the greens. Season with pepper and several shakes of soy sauce. They may even need a little salt as well. Try them and see.

Add a little oyster sauce, about three or four tablespoons. When all is hot and bubbling, eat immediately.

Masala onion spinach

For 2 as a side dish
2 onions, thinly sliced
groundnut oil
2 tablespoons dried coconut
a teaspoon of chilli powder
a tablespoon of ground coriander
a tablespoon of garam masala
a knife point of ground turmeric
2 garlic cloves, crushed
2 tablespoons lemon juice
500g (about 4 large double
     handfuls) spinach

Cook the onions in a little oil until soft and golden brown. This will take about ten minutes in a shallow pan set over a moderate heat. Mix the next seven ingredients together and add just enough water to form a rough, sloppy paste. Stir this spice paste into the cooked onions.

Wash the spinach and remove any tough stalks. Shred or tear the leaves into manageable pieces, unless they are small, in which case leave them whole. Dump them, still wet from the tap, into a large pan over a moderate heat. Cover tightly with a lid and cook for a minute or two until the spinach has softened.

Drain the spinach, put it on a hot plate, then tip the spiced onions over. Eat straight away.

Corn on the cob

Fantastic stuff. Buy young, proud, explicit cobs with their sheath still on, and plump, tightly packed kernels underneath. Size matters. Avoid anything withered. Peel off the papery skin, then throw them whole into boiling salted water and cook at an excited boil till a tested kernel comes away easily. It could take anything from five to fifteen minutes, depending on size and freshness. It should be as sweet as a nut. Smother the cob with melted butter and eat immediately, holding it in your hands, the butter dribbling down your chin. A feast.

Courgettes

Cheap, neat and quick to cook, the courgette has won its place on our shopping lists. Slicing half a dozen of the things quickly with your favourite small knife is pure therapy compared to hammering away for entrance to its older sister, the marrow. But are they really worth eating? Do courgettes actually taste of anything?

Boiled, I would suggest that they are no more interesting than boiled cucumber. But try this:

Slow-cooked courgettes with lemon and basil

For 2–4 as an accompaniment to a grill or roast, or perhaps fish cakes
half a dozen small courgettes
olive oil, a good fruity one
a juicy lemon
basil leaves, a handful (about 20)

Slice the courgettes at an angle, each one into about six pieces. Cutting at an angle exposes more of the flesh to the heat of the pan. Heat a little olive oil in a shallow pan, enough to cover the bottom and maybe a glug or two more. Then put in the sliced courgettes. Cover and cook over a low heat until the vegetables are golden and on their way to turning brown on their cut edges, about twenty minutes. You will need to toss them around from time to time.

Lift the vegetables out with a draining spoon. Squeeze the lemon juice into the pan. Scrape and stir in any sticky bits from the bottom. Throw in the basil leaves, torn up a bit. Salt and pepper it. Slosh the juices over the courgettes and eat hot.

Aubergines

The aubergine is the sexiest of vegetables, just as a ripe fig is the sexiest of fruits. Both of them, coincidentally, purple. But while a fig will tempt us straight from the tree, the aubergine is nothing till cooked. Bland and even bitter when raw, it is transformed when roasted, grilled or fried, into a subtly flavoured, slushy, juicy mass. Heat does the aubergine proud, performing what is little short of magic on its spongy, raw flesh.

British cooks have come late to the aubergine – we probably tried to boil it – and only in the last few years have paid it the attention it enjoys in the Middle East and the Mediterranean. There it is stuffed with onions and tomatoes, spiced with cumin, and beaten into garlicky purées. The purple-black jobby on sale in the greengrocer's is only one of several varieties that range from creamy white to black, and from golf ball to baseball bat. They are quite irresistible to caress. The most endearing are those that resemble the eggs that give the aubergine its American name of eggplant – their matt skin the colour of double cream. The tastiest seem to me to be the long lavender and ivory ones, curling back on themselves, looking like the magician's shoes from some Middle Eastern fairy story. The glossy Dutch dongs are a definite second best.

The aubergine takes up oil like a sponge takes water. But once it is cooked and cool, the oil will seep out again. So much oil is retained in the vegetable's cooked flesh that it is essential you use the best. Good olive oil – by which I mean fruity and brightly flavoured – is the minimum. While I normally hesitate to recommend cooking with extra virgin oil (it can be heavy and bullish in some recipes), I am the first to suggest it for frying an aubergine or for brushing thick slices prior to grilling. The oil becomes an integral part of the aubergine, changing its character and texture. This is not the time to stint.

An aubergine is supper rather than an accompaniment. Satisfying as beefsteak, rich as cream, yet light on the gut – if not the pocket. Grilled and eaten with salad leaves and garlic mayonnaise, baked till it collapses and eats like the tenderest meat, or fried like chips and sprinkled with a little too much salt, this majestic vegetable, technically a fruit, is at last finding a welcome in British kitchens. The aubergine is working its magic on us.

Roast aubergines

For 4 as a side dish
2 large aubergines, or a handful
    of smaller ones
olive oil
juice of 2 lemons
8 whole garlic cloves

A chuck-it-in-the-pan type of accompaniment.

Cut the aubergines into large chunks; bite-sized or a bit bigger. Put them in a roasting tin and pour over enough olive oil to wet them thoroughly and leave a puddle in the bottom of the tin. Squeeze in the lemon juice and add the garlic cloves, but squash them a bit first.

Roast in a hot oven (200°C/400°F/Gas 6), tossing the aubergines around the pan from time to time and pouring over more oil if necessary. They should be tender in about thirty minutes. Season with coarse salt.

Cream of roasted aubergine with garlic, mint and cumin

For 2
a large, fat aubergine or two,
    medium-sized
3 plump, juicy garlic cloves
a teaspoon of cumin seeds
olive oil – about 5 tablespoons
juice of a large lemon
finely chopped mint leaves, about
    a small palmful

Warm pitta bread is the best way to get this smoky, slippery dip into your mouth.

Put the aubergine and unpeeled garlic cloves in a roasting tin and bake in a hot oven (200°C/400°F/Gas 6) until soft and on the verge of collapse. (The aubergine, that is, not you.) After about forty-five minutes remove and allow to cool enough to handle. Meanwhile, toast the cumin seeds for a minute in a shallow pan, until they smell fragrant and darken slightly. Crush them to a powder with a pestle and mortar or an improvisation of such (a flat-ended rolling-pin and a pudding basin will do the trick).

Slice the aubergine in half and scoop out the flesh into a food processor if you have one, a large bowl if you don't. Squeeze the garlic out of its skin. Crush the flesh of both to a smoothish slush either with the processor blade or with a fork.

Beat in enough olive oil to turn the purée to a sloppy, but not runny, sludge. Season quite generously with salt, lemon juice, chopped mint and the cumin. Set aside for half an hour, or more if you can. Scoop up with warm pitta bread.

Roast spiced aubergines

An easy supper that demonstrates perfectly the aubergine's affinity with olive oil and spices.

Slice the aubergines in half lengthways. Make half a dozen deep diagonal slashes across each flat side, almost, but not quite, cutting through to the skin. Repeat at the opposite angle, to give a diamond effect. This will allow the heat to penetrate and the aubergine to cook much more quickly.

Scatter the surface of each half with salt and set aside, upside down, for a good half hour. Don't feel compelled to do this if you don't have time – but it will help the aubergine to soak up less oil. Once the vegetable has 'relaxed', rinse off the salt and pat dry. Place the aubergine halves in a roasting tin, skin side down, drizzle with a little oil, and bake in a hot oven, 200°C/400°F/Gas 6, until soft to the touch and on the verge of deflating. About forty minutes or so.

While they are cooking, grind the three seeds finely in a pestle and mortar or a coffee grinder. You can use pre-ground spices but you will miss much of their magic. Cook the three spices with the onions and garlic in a little olive oil until the onions are soft and rich gold in colour. Do this over a low heat and expect it to take at least twenty minutes. A sticky goo forming on the bottom of the pan is a bonus but don't let the onions burn.

When the aubergines are cooked, remove from the oven and turn them over. Add the chopped coriander and a little chilli powder to the onions, season with salt and lemon juice and stir in enough extra virgin olive oil to make an oniony slush. Scrape at the sticky goo on the bottom of the pan and stir it in. Spoon the spiced onion mixture over the aubergines, letting it run down into the splits. Serve warm, with a slick of thin yoghurt drizzled over.

For 2

2 large aubergines

olive oil

a teaspoonful of each of the following spices: cumin seeds, coriander seeds, cardamom seeds

4 medium-sized onions, roughly chopped

2 large cloves of garlic, thinly sliced

chopped coriander, a palmful, or basil if you prefer

ground chilli – a knife point or more if you wish

lemon juice

6 tablespoons natural yoghurt, stirred till it thins a little

Grilled Parmesan aubergines

aubergines (allow 1 per person)
extra virgin olive oil
grated Parmesan cheese (4 or 5
   tablespoons per aubergine)

A light lunch or supper.

Slice the aubergines into four or five long, thick tongues, from stalk downwards. If you have time, and wish to save olive oil, then scatter the slices with a little salt and leave them to drain and soften.

Get the grill hot. This is easiest cooked under an overhead grill. Rinse the aubergines if you have salted them, and brush them with olive oil. Be generous. Cook the slices until they are soft and golden brown. A matter of six or seven minutes, turning them once to cook the other side for slightly less.

Scatter the aubergines with the grated Parmesan (you won't need more than a tablespoon per slice), then return to the grill for a minute or so, keeping a beady watch on them. Parmesan burns in seconds. A tomato salad and some bread are fitting accompaniments.

Pesto aubergines

aubergines – 1 per person
extra virgin olive oil
pesto – 5 tablespoons per
   aubergine

Slice the aubergines into long, thick slices, about four or five per aubergine. Brush them generously with oil, a good fruity one, and put them under a hot grill. When they are soft and golden, after about six or seven minutes, then turn them over and cook the other side for five minutes or so. The slices should be tender and limp, soft enough to cut with a fork. Smear the slices with pesto, about a tablespoon per slice, and return to the grill till the pesto has melted a little and is just starting to bubble. Serve immediately.

Grilled aubergines with lemon salsa verde

Slice the aubergine lengthways into long steaks. Sprinkle with salt and allow to stand for half an hour, while you make the salsa verde and pour yourself a little drink. Rinse the aubergines gently, then pat them dry. Brush with olive oil and place on a hot grill pan, the ridged sort that sits over the hob. You can cook them under a grill, as in the previous recipe, if you wish. When they are tender on both sides and appetisingly charred in patches, then lift them off the grill on to warm plates.

To make the sauce, chop the herbs quite finely, but not so small that they look like tea leaves, then stir in the garlic, mustard and capers. Pour in the olive oil quite slowly, beating with a fork. Stir in the lemon juice and season with sea salt and black pepper. Be generous with the seasoning, tasting as you go. The sauce should be bouncy and piquant.

Spoon the sauce over and around the cooked aubergines and serve hot or warm.

For 2, as a light meal with, say, a tomato salad and bread
1 large aubergine

For the salsa verde:
a generous handful of parsley leaves
6 bushy sprigs of mint
a handful of basil leaves
2 cloves of garlic, crushed
a tablespoon or so of Dijon mustard
2 tablespoons capers, rinsed
6 tablespoons extra virgin olive oil
2 tablespoons lemon juice

Baked aubergines with crème fraîche and basil

Cut the aubergines into thin slices, about five or six per fruit. Fry the slices in a little oil in a shallow pan. When they are golden on both sides and quite relaxed, then lay them in a dish – a small gratin dish or shallow ovenproof casserole is fine. Tear the basil leaves up a bit and stir them into the crème fraîche with a seasoning of salt and pepper. Spoon the seasoned cream over the aubergines and bake in a hot oven at 200°C/400°F/Gas 6. After fifteen or twenty minutes they will be bubbling and aromatic. Serve as a light supper with crusty bread and a pudding afterwards, or as a side dish for grilled meat or chicken.

For 2
2 large aubergines
olive oil
a large handful of basil leaves
500ml pot of crème fraîche

Tomatoes

We eat far too many tomatoes. Instead of enjoying them only at their seasonal prime – sweet, tart and dripping with juice – we buy them all year round, somehow convinced that they are essential to our cooking. They are not. At the height of summer, their seedy jelly all tart and slippery, dressed simply with green oil and scrunched-up basil leaves, they are worth calling lunch. Some are even interesting enough to munch in the hand like an apple or a peach. Come winter, when the only toms on offer are imported ones, all flat and dull, you might as well buy a tin.

In summer I do very little with the fruit, letting it rub shoulders only with its closest friends – salt, anchovies, olives or cheese, mild, sweet onions, olive oil, basil or oregano. Don't bother to go beyond this, little will come of it. In winter when the fruit comes from a bottle or tin, then a little more effort may be worth the trouble.

Tomatoes with olive oil and basil

Slice the tomatoes – not so thinly that you can see through them – and lay them on a plate. I use small, oval, white plates for this sort of thing. Drizzle over a little olive oil (the quality of the oil is make or break) and scatter over a few basil leaves, shredded or crushed in the hand. A little salt or pepper, both freshly crushed, is a worthwhile addition, but only after you have tasted the salad. Sometimes it will need neither.

For 2
half a dozen perfectly ripe,
   luscious tomatoes
extra virgin olive oil (a fruity,
   peppery one)
basil leaves – a handful

Roast tomatoes

Cut a deep cross in the tomatoes, push in a small lump of butter and some shredded basil leaves and season with a grinding of salt and black pepper. Roast at 200°C/400°F/Gas 6, until the butter is bubbling and the tomatoes are meltingly soft – about twenty minutes. Serve while still hot and fragrant.

tomatoes
butter
basil

Roast tomato salad

For 2

6 medium-sized ripe tomatoes

2 plump cloves of garlic,
  squashed

6 anchovy fillets, rinsed of their
  salt or oil

a good handful of basil leaves

olive oil, probably about 100ml

Roasting concentrates the flavour of the fruit. It may even perk up a slightly dull-tasting one.

Cut the tomatoes in half and place, cut-side up, in an ovenproof dish. Put in a hot oven and roast at 200°C/400°F/Gas 6 until soft and about to collapse, about twenty minutes. Meanwhile, crush the garlic, anchovies, basil and some salt and coarsely ground pepper to a thick slush with the olive oil. A pestle and mortar, blender or simply a basin and wooden spoon will do.

When the tomatoes come out of the oven, pour over the dressing and serve while still warm, with bread to mop up the juices.

Baked tomatoes with garlic and crumbs

For 2–4 as a light meal

6 ripe or almost ripe tomatoes

3 cloves of garlic, crushed

a large handful of parsley leaves,
  chopped

a handful of breadcrumbs

olive oil

grated Parmesan cheese

A sort of throw-it-in-the-oven supper for a summer's evening.

Slice the tomatoes in half around their circumference, unless they are those oval plum numbers, in which case it is easier to cut from stem end down. Push out most of the seeds with your finger. Mix the crushed garlic, chopped parsley and breadcrumbs together and season with a hefty grinding of pepper and salt. Stuff the filling into the hollows in the tomato halves. The tomatoes should be pretty much covered. Drizzle over a little olive oil, just a glug into each tomato, then sprinkle liberally with Parmesan cheese.

Bake in a preheated oven at 200°C/400°F/Gas 6 until the cheese is starting to turn an appetising golden brown; about thirty minutes, maybe a little less. Serve warm.

Mushrooms

There can be magic in a mushroom. But only if cooked simply with butter, pepper, parsley and onion. Maybe a bit of tarragon or cheese, but nothing fancy. The best you will ever eat will be one cooked on a camp-fire in the woods. *Haute cuisine* is the death knell to fungi. In my own kitchen the mushroom has long been treated as one of the most worthwhile ingredients – savoury, slippery, sweet nuggets that often season a stew or a plate of pasta but are really better eaten on their own. Just ignore everything you read about mushroom mousse, roulade or soufflé being good to eat – they rarely are. Don't mess with a mushroom.

Sometimes mushrooms can be almost beefy. If you don't believe me, then soak a dried porcini in warm water and taste the resulting broth. Fresh mushrooms, especially the large dark brown-gilled ones as big as your hand, mature wonderfully in a paper bag in the salad drawer of the fridge. After a day or two they smell like autumn woods after the rain and their flavour will be deeper than when they are shop-fresh. Though they will turn to slime if you use a plastic bag.

Chestnut mushrooms, sliced thickly and fried with butter, garlic and parsley till they are caramel brown and savoury-sweet in the mouth, are probably the most underrated of platefuls. With bread, this makes a light supper, enough if there is soup before or pudding to follow, and wine bold enough to take the lightly cooked garlic. Without the garlic it is Sunday breakfast from heaven.

Fancy fungi

A lot of fancy mushrooms taste little different from the common or garden variety. A fat porcini can be worth the money, but only if you find one that isn't full of holes. Even the poshest of emporiums sell mushrooms in poor nick. But when they are sound and heavy to the touch, and in perfect condition, they are worth the price of admission. Do little with them. Cook them gently with butter, black pepper and a little chopped parsley in a shallow pan. Nothing more than that.

A mushroom sauté

For 2

a generous knob of butter, about 25g

2 finely chopped cloves of garlic

olive oil, about 3 tablespoons

4 handfuls of mushrooms/about 450g

a small handful of chopped parsley

lemon

Any old mushroom is suitable for this treatment.

Warm the butter in a shallow pan. When it starts to sizzle, add the chopped garlic. Cook till soft, stirring so that it does not colour, then add the oil. When it bubbles, toss in the mushrooms, which should be quartered, or at least chopped up a bit, and half the parsley. The thickness is immaterial – the thinner they are sliced, the quicker they will cook. Though I make a plea for thick slices – they finish their cooking a little juicier. They will drink the butter and the oil quickly, and you may need to add just a little more.

When the mushrooms are coloured here and there and smell tempting, add the remaining parsley. Toss the mushrooms round the pan for a minute or two, season with salt, then eat straight away, with a squeeze of lemon if you like. This is one of those things that beg to be eaten from plain white plates.

Mushroom and onion sauté

For 2 as a side dish

1 medium-sized onion, cut into
    thin rings
3 tablespoons olive oil
butter
750g mushrooms (any sort),
    sliced
a small handful of chopped
    parsley

Cook the sliced onion in the olive oil and a little melted butter until golden and soft. A matter of about ten minutes over a moderate heat. It must be fully cooked though, before you add the mushrooms.

Toss the sliced mushrooms and cook, adding a little more oil and butter if they look at all dry, until the mushrooms are golden and interesting. Season with salt and stir in the parsley.

Slow-baked mushrooms

For 2

6 large flat mushrooms
a large lump of butter, about 50g
soy sauce
a juicy lemon
4 tablespoons olive oil or half
    olive and walnut

A huge, flat mushroom, all dark-brown velvet gills and as big as your hand, is as good as a slice of beefsteak to some. I shall not argue, being more of a fan of fungi than flesh. You can grill them, which means constantly anointing with oil, fry them in a pan or bake them in the oven. Either way they will drink all your olive oil. Try slow cooking them in the oven. Meltingly tender, deeply savoury and better than beef. Pure magic.

Put the mushrooms, wiped of any dirt, into a roasting tin. Dot with butter. Shake over a little soy sauce, about 2 tablespoons – how much is up to you. Squeeze over the juice from the lemon. Then drizzle with the olive oil. Bring to the boil over a medium heat, cover with a reasonably tight lid or tin foil, then put in a preheated oven (180°C/350°F/Gas 4).

Bake until the mushrooms are tender and juicy, about thirty to forty-five minutes, spooning the cooking liquor over them from time to time. Eat as a side dish with pretty much anything or, as I do, with buttered noodles, or mashed or fried potatoes.

Mushroom and spinach lasagne

This takes about an hour to prepare. Then there is half an hour in the oven but it is worth it – satisfying, earthy and rich. The sort of thing to stick on the table with a bowl of salad when friends come round. Dried lasagne, the type that requires no pre-cooking, is the stuff to buy. Don't turn your nose up either at the ready-made béchamel sauce sold in TetraPaks in Italian delis – it's good enough – and it saves dithering about making white sauce.

Wash the spinach thoroughly. Slice the mushrooms thickly without bothering to peel them or remove their stalks – it's all good stuff. Pour enough oil into a large deep pan to cover the bottom, three or four tablespoons. Add the chopped onions and cook over a moderate heat, stirring from time to time, until they are soft and translucent. While they are cooking, which will take a good fifteen minutes, peel and slice the garlic and stir it in with a few pinches of dried oregano and the bay leaves.

When all is soft, fragrant and sticky, stir in the sliced mushrooms and continue to cook, stirring occasionally, for ten or fifteen minutes or so. When the mushrooms and onions are dark and earthy and a flavoursome goo has built up in the pan, stir in the tomato purée and chopped tomatoes. Leave the sauce to cook over a low heat for about twenty minutes, adding salt and plenty of black pepper. You should end up with a wet, dark, meaty slush.

Meanwhile, take the wet spinach and dump it in a large pan over a moderate heat, and slam on the lid. It will cook in its own steam, provided it was wet when you put it in. Shake the pan once or twice to stop the leaves sticking. They will be soft but still bright in about three minutes. (I never cease to be amazed at how a big potful of spinach cooks down to nothing.) Drain in a colander.

If you are using the ready-made béchamel sauce, thin it a little with three or four tablespoons of milk or single cream. Put half the béchamel in a large baking dish (I use a deep oval Le Creuset about 30cm long), then add a layer of pasta (about three small sheets) breaking it up and fitting it in snugly. Spoon over a thick layer of the mushroom sauce, squeeze any water out of the spinach with your fist, then lay half of it over the sauce. Add layers of pasta, mushroom sauce and spinach, finishing with the béchamel. Scatter the Parmesan cheese over the top. Bake in a preheated oven at 190°C/375°F/Gas 5 until bubbling – about twenty-five minutes to half an hour.

For 4

400g fresh spinach
300g brown mushrooms
olive oil
3 medium-sized onions, roughly chopped
3 plump and juicy cloves of garlic
dried oregano
a couple of bay leaves
a good squeeze of tomato purée (about a tablespoon)
2 x 400g tins of tomatoes, crushed
500ml béchamel sauce
180g dried lasagne (about 9 of those little rectangles)
6 tablespoons grated Parmesan cheese

Onions, leeks, shallots and garlic

An onion is more than an aromatic with which to start a stew. An onion can be supper. A huge golden globe, glistening with butter and thyme – a hunk of cheese melting by its side, and a wedge of bread from a crusty loaf is supper enough for me. Though it wouldn't appeal to the meat-and-two-veg brigade.

Shallots, the elegant, oval onions – their golden-brown skins occasionally flushed with pink – can be roasted till their insides are soft enough to squeeze effortlessly out. Their slippery, translucent flesh makes a savoury partner for good, tough-crusted bread and a glass of wine. Once baked, their skins removed, it is nothing to toss them in cream and herbs and return them to the oven till bubbling.

The rich, sweet smell of onions, shallots or garlic baking in the oven, their edges caramelising in the heat, is enough to bring anyone to the table. A bowl of soup, a white dish of oven-roasted onions and a wedge of cheese is a far more luxurious meal than it sounds. If there are cooked onions in the fridge then pile them on to hot toast and cover with slices of cheese for the best of all cheese-on-toast snacks.

Fried onions, slithery, sugary and faintly burned at the edges, add a sweet, savoury note to supper. Even one as simple as a baked potato or sausages. They are no trouble, though the cook should peer at them from time to time as they melt slowly in their pan. Get them right – neither undercooked nor burned too much and they offer richness for little more than pennies.

The leek is the onion's more refined sister. Slim, sometimes almost pencil-thin, delicate and subtle – yet she can still be fun. It is the white flesh we want; the green leaves of the large leek are coarse, though they are pleasant enough in the very young. The ones you eat with your fingers like asparagus. This is not a pretension – they are just as good, sometimes more interesting, than the esteemed spears. Finicky cooks will use the leek's layers as an edible wrapper for all and sundry. But this book is about making something simple to eat, so I shall not suggest such things.

Shallots baked in their skins

The meaty, torpedo-shaped banana shallot is the most suitable for roasting, the other being too small to fiddle about with.

Make a deep cut along the length of each shallot, still in its skin, and pack them into a roasting tin. Scatter with thyme sprigs, drizzle with olive oil and bake in a hot oven (200°C/400°F/Gas 6) till they give when squeezed. Depending on your shallots, this will probably take about forty-five minutes. Remove them from the oven, serving them as they are, for everyone to help themselves, splitting the skins and teasing out the melting onion flesh. Smear with butter and eat while they are still hot with cheese (a lump of Caerphilly or Wensleydale would be appropriate while Cotherstone, mild but piquant, would be heaven) and some bread.

For 2 as a light supper
long shallots, about 12
thyme, a few sprigs
olive oil
butter and cheese to serve

Roast shallots with butter and thyme

For 2–4
shallots, about 8
butter
thyme leaves

Pink and gold and sweet and buttery.

Peel the shallots and halve lengthways, then place in a roasting tin or gratin dish. Dot generously with butter, probably about 50g or so, and scatter with thyme leaves, a palmful will do. If it is lemon thyme you have, so much the better. Roast in a hot oven (180°C/350°F/Gas 4), shaking the tin occasionally, until they are golden and buttery and meltingly tender. Expect them to take a good forty-five minutes to an hour. They must be tender enough to crush between your fingers, though the outside leaves should be crisp. Eat warm with bread for a snack, or as an accompaniment to, say, roast pork.

» Roasted with olive oil instead of butter, and the juices sharpened with a little lemon juice or vinegar at the end of cooking, this makes a very fine salad too.

Slow-roast onions with melted cheese

For 2, as a light supper
4 medium-sized onions
extra virgin olive oil
cheese

A lazy supper, though you will need a salad after. Probably a pudding, too.

Peel the onions, then cut a cross down from the top of each one to the root. Place them in a roasting tin of some sort and drizzle them with olive oil. A fruity oil is best if you have the choice. Place the onions, covered with foil, in a medium-hot oven (180°C/350°F/Gas 4) and roast for about forty-five minutes.

Remove the foil, spoon some of the oil over the onions and return them to the oven, without the foil, for a further fifteen minutes till golden and soft. Slice some cheese thinly. It honestly does not matter what sort it is, use whatever you have. Camembert is just as suitable as Cheddar, Gruyère as suitable as Cambazola. You can even use Edam, though I cannot think why you would have bought such a bland, rubbery thing. Place the cheese on top of the onions, as much or as little as you like, I suggest about 100g, then return them to the oven till the cheese has started to melt. Eat as soon as the cheese becomes molten.

Grilled leeks with a gutsy dressing

Wash the leeks under the cold tap to free any trapped grit or sand. Drop them into a pan of boiling, salted water. Leave till tender and slightly limp. About five minutes. Drain.

Heat a cast iron grill pan over a moderate heat. Smear the leeks with olive oil. Place them on the grill, in single file and barely touching. While they cook, whisk the mustard with the vinegar, a generous seasoning of salt and pepper and the rest of the oil.

Turn the leeks once and cook till soft and slightly charred. Lift them from the grill and put in a shallow dish. Pour the dressing over and leave till the leeks are warm, rather than hot. Eat with hunks of bread.

For 3 as a snack, 2 as a light lunch with soup or pudding
12 leeks, barely thicker than a finger
olive oil, about 150ml
a tablespoon of smooth Dijon mustard
a tablespoon of red wine vinegar

Cream of roast onion soup with Thai spices

Sweet, sour, hot and creamy. A soup to invigorate.

Cut the onions in half vertically, skin and all. Put in a baking tray, either way up, with the unpeeled garlic cloves. Roast in a hot oven (200°C/400°F/Gas 6) for forty-five minutes, turning once.

When the onions are golden and soft, peel off the skin and drop the flesh into a deep saucepan, separating some of the layers as you go. Add the roast garlic, popped out of its skin, the stock, fish sauce, shredded lime leaves, grated ginger and chillies. Bring to the boil, turn down the heat and simmer for about twenty minutes.

Stir in the coconut milk, bring back to simmering point, then taste for seasoning. It may need salt (or soy if you prefer). It should be sweet from the onions, sour from the lime, hot from the chillies and creamy from the coconut milk. Serve hot.

For 2–4
4 medium-sized onions
4 plump cloves of garlic
a litre of ready-made vegetable or chicken stock
Thai fish sauce (nam pla), about a tablespoon
6 lime leaves, rolled up tightly and shredded (or the grated zest and juice of a lime)
a lump of ginger, as big as a walnut, grated
2 small red chillies, seeded and chopped
400ml tin of coconut milk

Parsnips

The parsnip begs for spice. It begs for butter, too. It shares the sweetness common to all root vegetables but boasts a strength of flavour that will stand up to chilli, turmeric and mustard. It loves black pepper. Honey brings out its sweetness, cream cools it, salt makes it sing. Roasted, the parsnip is a sweet nugget to find sticky and caramelised under the beef; mashed, it gives a rich, fluffy pile on which to dump browned onions and buttery spice mixtures.

Thick, hard parsnips will have more flavour, especially if they have seen a frost, than those from the nursery slopes. But they will need peeling. The baby versions, neat in their plastic coffins from the supermarket, lack guts. Leave them be, and for once go for the big guys. If there are parsnips needing to be used, or (more to the point) there is little else for supper, then look to the spice shelf. If there is mustard, cayenne or a jar of spice paste then you have the making of the most comforting soup of all. If there is cheese (even hard and dry) to grate into it – then you have a feast.

Mashed parsnips with spiced butter and bacon

For 2 as an accompaniment
2 large, fat parsnips
butter, about 75g
bacon or pancetta, about 100g, diced
a large onion, sliced
a tablespoon of grain mustard
a palmful of chopped mint leaves
a tablespoon of garam masala

Wipe the parsnips, peeling them if the skins are coarse. Cut them up a bit, then boil them until tender in salted water – a matter of about fifteen minutes. They are ready when you can squash them against the side of the pan. Drain and mash with a potato masher or fork.

While the parsnips are cooking, melt the butter in a shallow pan and sizzle the bacon in it for a minute or two. When the bacon fat is golden brown, add the sliced onion and continue cooking, on a moderate heat, for about ten minutes, till soft and golden, sweet and translucent. Stir in the mustard, mint leaves and the garam masala. Cook for a minute, then stir in the mashed parsnip. Press down into the pan and leave to cook until the underside has caught golden brown in patches. Evenness is not important, it is just the odd crusty patch we are after. Serve straight away, perhaps with cold cuts.

Pan-fried parsnips with browned shallots, garlic and spices

For 2, as an accompaniment or light lunch dish. Great with sausages

2 medium-sized parsnips

butter, a walnut-sized lump, plus a little more later

3 tablespoons olive oil

2 large shallots, thinly sliced

2 cloves of garlic, thinly sliced

a whole dried chilli

a teaspoonful of coriander seeds, lightly crushed

8 cardamom pods

2 curry leaves

If the oven is on anyway, then you could roast this dish instead. Put it in once you have added the parsnips to the shallots, then roast for half an hour in a hot oven till the parsnips are almost falling to pieces.

Wipe or scrub the parsnips thoroughly, cut them into thick slices and boil them in salted water till very tender – a matter of fifteen minutes. Drain. Put the butter and the oil in a shallow pan and warm over a moderate heat. Add the shallots and garlic and cook until rich gold and translucent. A good ten minutes, maybe longer. Add the spices and curry leaves and season with both salt and freshly ground black pepper. Pepper is often a good idea with parsnips. Add the drained parsnips and a little more butter. Continue cooking, the heat turned up a little, until all is golden – about ten minutes – and lightly crisp and crumbly here and there.

Carrots

It is the carrots' colour, admittedly a welcome flash in the drab winter vegetable rack, that makes them as popular as peas. They have never intrigued me the way parsnips or beetroot do, and I prefer to crunch them raw, wet from the cold tap. Winter carrots, their flavour rich, their flesh hard, interest me more than the much-prized finger-sized spring variety. A big one, munched raw till your gums ache, is a good cure for a hangover. At least it will make your mouth feel better.

It is only since I swapped their cooking water for oil and butter and their chopped parsley garnish for a seasoning of Indian spices that my interest in the carrot has been aroused. It remains just that, though; an interest rather than a passion.

Roast carrots with bacon

Give the carrots a good wipe and cut them into chunks. The size is immaterial to the finished dish but it will affect the cooking time. I suggest about the size of a cork. Cut the onion into segments, about eight. Dice the bacon. Melt the butter in a roasting tin and toss the carrots, onion and diced bacon in it, then season with black pepper and put into a hot oven (200°C/400°F/Gas 6) for about half an hour. Shake the tin from time to time. The carrots are ready when tender to the point of a knife and golden brown at the edges.

For 2 as an accompaniment
carrots, 3 or 4 large ones
a medium-sized onion, peeled
2 handfuls (about 100g) of
  smoked streaky bacon or
  pancetta
butter, a lump as big as a walnut

Carrots with cumin and lemon

Good with pork, roast or grilled.

Cut the carrots into cork-sized pieces and put them in a deep saucepan. Pour in enough stock to come half-way up them, then add the other ingredients. You had better put some salt in, too. Bring them to the boil, then turn the heat down a little so that they continue to cook at a vigorous bubble. Cover with a lid. After ten to fifteen minutes they will be tender but have a bit of bite left in them. In which case they will be ready to eat.

For 2 as an accompaniment
3 or 4 large carrots
ready-made chicken or vegetable
  stock
juice and zest of a lemon
2 bay leaves
a teaspoon of cumin seeds

Beetroot

The beet's magenta orb deserves a better fate than to be boiled, sliced and vinegared for the British picnic. Beetroot roasts sweetly, its flavour deepening in the oven. The smaller the better – tastes the same, but takes half the time to cook. Leave those larger than a pomegranate for the people who pickle. Go for the babies barely bigger than a light bulb. We will roast them with spice, fry them with capers and dress them with yoghurt, tempering their generous dose of sugar with a splash of sourness. Though baked and buttered they are good with ham – but better with pastrami.

Don't be tempted to buy the cooked ones. They will have lost their joy and gained an E number – or, worse still, a dash of vinegar. I must make a plea for grated beetroot – rich and sweet when fried in butter, clean and refreshing when tossed raw with lemon juice and mint. Providing you don't mind pink teeth. Oh, and don't wear white when dealing with beetroot – or anything that won't look better sporting fingerprints of deepest garnet red.

Buttered beetroot

For 2
6 small beetroot
butter

Wash the beets, taking care not to split the skin. Wrap them loosely in foil and roast for about an hour in a hot oven (200°C/400°F/Gas 6). The larger your beets, the longer they will take to cook. Take them from the oven and unwrap them, split them open and stuff a thick slice of butter into each hot beet. Eat while the butter is melting. At its best as a side dish for cold roast beef or pork.

Roast balsamic beetroot

Wash the beetroot without splitting the skins or removing the stems. Put in a deep saucepan and cover with water, then bring to the boil, turn down and leave at a rolling boil till tender. Depending on the size of your beetroot, allow about thirty minutes for this. Drain and peel when they are soft enough to be pierced easily with a knife point.

Peel away the skins, cut each beet into six wedges and toss them in a roasting tin with a little olive oil. Cut the onions into segments from root to tip, about six from each onion. Add them to the beetroot and cover the tin with foil. Roast in a hot oven (200°C/400°F/Gas 6) for thirty minutes. Remove the foil, add a sprinkling of balsamic vinegar – not too much; only enough to add a little mellowness and depth – and a little salt. Return to the oven for a further thirty minutes, this time without the foil, until the vegetables are tender and brown at the edges.

For 2 as an accompaniment, perhaps to a cold roast
6 small beetroot, with stems if
    possible
a little olive oil, about 2
    tablespoons
2 medium-sized onions, peeled
balsamic vinegar, a little

Jerusalem artichokes

Jerusalem artichokes are the knobbly beige tubers whose reputation for making you fart far outshines their reputation for making velvety soups, sweetly melting roasts and nutty, gentle salads. I cannot understand why they are not more popular – especially as I have a theory that everyone secretly enjoys a good fart.

It may be my imagination but I am convinced that Jerusalem artichokes are not as knobbly as they were. Growers are probably producing the less lumpy varieties – which is good news for those who avoided them because they were a bugger to peel. Let's hope that that is all the growers tinker with. I hear that there is research being done to reduce their flatulence factor. In the States apparently. Some people have no sense of humour.

Jerusalems should be plump and hard, not wizened as I so often see them. You don't have to be too fussy about peeling them; a bit of skin here and there is of no consequence. One of those loose-handled traditional vegetable peelers is the tool for the job. It is not essential to peel them, but as the skin toughens on cooking, might I suggest ten minutes at the sink with a peeler.

This tuber has an affinity with scallops, with bacon and with chopped parsley – lots of it and not too finely chopped either. Butter, rather than oil, is the most suitable fat. It seems to tease out their sweetness. The tenderest of the roots, they will roast, purée and sauté. But they bore when boiled. If you have never tried them I beg you to give them a go – they are not expensive and if you don't like their taste – which is unlikely – at least you might enjoy their after-effects.

Roast artichokes

For about 4 as a side dish
artichokes, about 500g
two lemons
butter and olive oil
sprigs of thyme and bay

Scrub the artichokes clean under running water. Cut them in half and sit them in a roasting tin. Squeeze over the juice of two lemons. Dot the tubers with butter and pour over enough olive oil just to cover the base of the tin. Tuck the lemon shells and a few sprigs of thyme and bay among the artichokes. Roast at 190°C/375°F/Gas 5 until the artichokes' ivory flesh is soft and their skin is all gooey and sticky underneath, about forty-five minutes.

Buttered artichokes with thyme and garlic

Peel the artichokes. Melt the butter in a shallow pan, one to which you have a lid. Drop the garlic cloves, whole and unpeeled, the bay leaves, thyme leaves and a little coarsely ground black pepper into the butter. Add the artichokes and cook over a moderate heat until the artichokes and garlic are golden here and there. Take great care not to let the butter burn. If it looks as if it might then pour in a little olive oil.

Turn the heat down so that the butter is just lightly bubbling rather than sizzling, cover with a lid, then leave to cook for about fifteen minutes. Shake the pan two or three times as they cook. Remove the lid, turn the heat up again and continue cooking till the artichokes are meltingly tender, golden and crusty. As you eat the Jerusalems, squash the garlic cloves with your knife and spread a little of the sweet insides on each piece of buttery, sticky artichoke.

For 2 as an accompaniment, especially good with roast beef, pork and chicken

500g Jerusalem artichokes (3 or 4 big handfuls)
butter, about 75g
8 cloves of garlic
a couple of bay leaves
the leaves of 4 bushy sprigs of thyme

Artichoke soup with garlic butter

Peel the artichokes. You can be a bit sloppy about this – a little skin left on the very knobbly ones won't hurt. Wipe the artichokes thoroughly but don't bother to peel them. Cut them up a bit, then put them in a pan with the roughly chopped onion and the butter. Cover with a lid and stew the vegetables in the butter for ten minutes, until they are golden and soft, giving them the occasional shake.

Pour in enough water to cover them completely; it will probably be about half a litre. Salt. Now leave to cook, bubbling contentedly rather than boiling furiously, until the artichokes are soft. That is slightly more than tender, and will probably take about twenty minutes.

Whiz the whole lot in the blender till smooth. It will be beige flecked with brown. Pour it back into the saucepan and add pepper and salt. Be generous with both. Mash the butter with the crushed garlic and the chopped parsley. Add the cream to the soup and bring to the boil. Ladle into bowls and add a dollop of garlic butter to each. Crusty bread to serve.

For 4

500g Jerusalem artichokes, (3 or 4 big handfuls)
an onion, roughly chopped
75g butter
a small pot of double cream

For the butter:

50g butter, at room temperature
2 cloves of garlic, crushed to a mush with a little salt
a palmful of parsley sprigs, chopped

Buried treasure

Unctuous *pommes Dauphinoise*, thick with cream and garlic; crisp-shelled potato cakes hot from the pan; mountains of mash; sticky and melting spuds gooey from around the roast; and chips – thick ones fried in butcher's dripping – the friendliest, most comforting food in the world.

Even a single potato is a friend to the hungry. Wet it and rub it with salt, then bake till the skin is crisp and the flesh is fluffy and white. Crack it open and slide in some butter. Comfort food of the highest order. A baked potato is a hot water bottle you can eat.

A soothing potato cake, a little patty of docile mash bound with flour and gently browned, is a nice enough thing to find on your plate when jazzy flavours become too much. A dish of buttered mash, topped with slivers of onion fried with garam masala spices and butter, marries the bland to the fragrant, while those in search of an instant fix find consolation in a bag of salted crisps.

Those who fancy the tight, neat shape and freshly dug flavour of a new potato may have to grow their own now that so much of what is for sale is nothing more than immature King Edwards – commerce missing the point again. Those who put flavour before francs will happily part with the king's ransom asked for Jersey Royals in their wooden caskets of sand.

But what is a potato without fat? Or any starch for that matter? Where is the joy, the comfort, the sex appeal in a white, naked, steamed potato? Food for the fragile. The spud succeeds only where it meets up with fat – butter, olive oil, cream, meat juices, bacon or dripping. A spud's simple starch needs enriching, though not necessarily to excess. A roll in a pool of melted butter or gravy is enough to give point to even the plainest of boiled tubers.

I will not mess around with a spud. The classic dishes cannot be bettered by any meddling whiz-kid. *Pommes Anna*, thinly sliced and baked with butter to the point of collapse; *pommes boulangère*, tatties cooked in stock so that they are crisp on top and soggy and savoury underneath; or bubble and squeak, those all too rare patties of mashed potato and shredded dark green cabbage. Once mastered, you cannot beat them, so why try?

To deny a potato its lubricant of fat is seriously to misunderstand the vegetable. New potatoes dipped, still steaming and salty from their cooking water, into sharp crème fraîche; warm, waxy salad spuds, sliced into stiff mayo; or those mountains of mash with their pool of melting butter at their summit – food fit for the gods.

Potatoes

My passion for the potato never dims. Especially for the fat, yellow, floury ones for baking or mash. I have been known to boil a pile of them to eat with yesterday's gravy from the roast, piping hot and highly seasoned. Smashing them into the pan drippings with my fork. A baked potato, butter dribbling down its salt-crusted skin, is not an accompaniment to supper for me – it *is* supper. I hold the highest respect and greatest affection for the humble spud. I suspect I always will.

Of course the potato is as much about texture as flavour. More, in fact, though the difference in flavour between a tattie just dug from the garden and one that has been sweating in a plastic bag at the local shop is not to be underestimated.

The texture of a potato decrees its use. Where a firm, creamy texture is wanted, in salads or for sautéing, a small waxy potato is to be suggested, such as Charlotte or Diana. Where a fluffy texture is the whole point, for baking or mash for instance, then a mealy, floury potato such as King Edward, Maris Piper or Wilja is more suitable. Having said that, you can use whatever type of potato comes to hand. The difference will be minimal, unless you decide to make mash with waxy potatoes and end up with glue.

Potato salad

The waxy-fleshed potato, invariably smaller than the floury-fleshed one, is a richer eat. The most common varieties are Charlotte and the Pink Fir Apple. They are the ones the supermarkets have decided we should eat. The quintessential salad potato, often boiled and sliced into mayonnaise with spring onion and parsley. To be honest, I prefer a potato salad made with a floury variety, finding the buttery texture of a traditional salad spud too cloying once dressed with an oily mayo. But that is being fussy.

A bright, sassy sauce of oil, lemon, capers and parsley seems much more suitable. Dressing the potatoes while they are hot will ensure they soak up the liquid, becoming generously drenched with seasonings.

Waxy potato salad

Bring a deep pan of water to the boil. Salt it and add the potatoes, wiped if at all dusty or muddy. When the water returns to the boil, turn the heat down slightly to a soft boil. You might say a jolly boil rather than a furious one. When the potatoes are tender to the point of a knife, after about twelve to fifteen minutes or so, they are done. Drain them and cut each in half.

In a small bowl whisk about 4 tablespoons of the oil with a good pinch or two of sea salt and three or four grinds of pepper. The salt should dissolve. Add a few capers, about ten or so, then squeeze in the juice of the lemon. Mix in the chopped parsley. You will have a thick, oily, green sludge. Tip it over the potatoes and toss gently. Leave for ten minutes or so for the dressing to be absorbed. Then eat, preferably before they cool.

For 2
2 handfuls of waxy-fleshed
  potatoes (about 16 small ones)
olive oil – green and fruity
capers, a tablespoon or so, rinsed
a lemon
a handful of coarsely chopped
  parsley

Pommes Dauphinoise

For 4

4 medium-sized potatoes, waxy-
 fleshed if possible
a large clove of plump, juicy
 garlic
butter
100ml milk
100ml double cream

Luxurious, indulgent and calming, the potato gratin is the most sen-suous of dishes. Thinly sliced potatoes are baked slowly with cream and garlic, a flattering partner to a plate of roast lamb. Part of my wandering apprenticeship found me preparing six dishes a day for a West Country castle-turned-restaurant, the mild scent of slow-cooked garlic wafting through the grey stone corridors. The secret, according to my mentor, is to cook the dauph (as it was known) in the slowest oven – till the potato slices almost disintegrate.

Peel the potatoes and slice them thinly. No thicker than one pound coins. Thinner if possible. You may read elsewhere to soak the slices in water – don't. Rub a gratin dish or roasting tin with the garlic. Eas-iest done by cutting the clove in half and pressing hard as you wipe the inside of the dish with it. Its juices will ooze out. Smear the dish gen-erously with butter.

Lay the potato slices in the dish – neatly or hugger-mugger, it mat-ters not a jot – then mix the milk and cream together and season with salt and pepper. Pour the mixture into the dish. It should just come to the top of the potatoes. If it doesn't, add a little more cream and milk.

Bake the dauphinoise in a warm oven (170°C/325°F/Gas 3) for about an hour, maybe an hour and a half, until they are truly tender – almost melting. The cooking time will depend on the type and thick-ness of the potato.

Pot-roast potatoes

Slice the onions finely. Warm the olive oil and the butter in a deep ovenproof pot until the butter melts, then throw in the sliced onions. Cover with a lid and cook until the onions are soft, about ten minutes. Move them around the pan from time to time to stop them sticking. Though some stickiness is a bonus – that is partly where the flavour comes from.

Slice the potatoes thinly, without bothering to peel them, and place them in the pot in rough layers with the onions and a couple of bay leaves plus a doubly generous seasoning of salt and pepper. Pour in enough water or stock to come most of the way up the potatoes and onions. Bake in a hot oven (190°C/375°F/Gas 5) until the potatoes are fork tender, perhaps even a little crumbly.

For 2–4

4 medium-sized onions, peeled
olive oil, a little
butter, a thick slice
4 large potatoes (any sort)
bay leaves
500ml water or stock (any type)

Pan-fried

I have a soft spot for the frying pan. I had little else when I arrived in London all those years ago. Potatoes fried till they develop a crisp and golden crust, or cooked slowly in thin layers till meltingly tender. Sauté potatoes, the flat discs of spud that come to the table unannounced in French restaurants (the sort with white paper tablecloths, starchy waitresses and well-worn white china, where no one asks to see the menu). One of my favourite suppers is yesterday's boiled potatoes sliced up and fried till crisp, then eaten with slices and lumps hacked off the cold roast joint.

Sauté potatoes

For 4

450g potatoes, floury or waxy, not too large
butter or beef dripping
olive oil

A sauté potato is a thinly sliced one that has been fried in butter. It is one of those things that demands to be eaten sprinkled with salt. Simplicity itself, and the perfect accompaniment to any creamily sauced fish or poultry. Good with steak too. Not surprisingly, they are considered a fiddle; you should use clarified butter and preferably pre-boiled and skinned potatoes. But we can cheat a little.

A small amount of oil added to the pan will stop the butter burning, giving much the same effect as clarified butter. The flavour will be little different if we use a light olive or groundnut oil. Waxy-fleshed potatoes, such as Charlotte or La Ratte, fry neatly without breaking. A floury potato, such as King Edwards, will be more tender in the pan, being difficult to turn, but will crumble and crisp appetisingly. The choice is ours.

Put the potatoes into a pan of boiling water and cook till almost tender. About ten minutes. Drain them and slip off the skins. Slice the potatoes. I suggest about 5mm thick. That is about as thick as two pound coins, which is much more my sort of measurement.

Melt a good-sized lump of butter or dripping, probably about 50g, in a shallow pan with a little oil. The quantity is not crucial, but there should be a layer of fat covering the bottom of the pan about 5mm thick. A heavy-bottomed pan will prevent uneven cooking. Bring the butter and oil up to the point where it starts to bubble, then add the sliced potatoes, enough to sit comfortably in a single layer in the pan. Then turn the heat down.

Cook until the underside of each potato is golden and crisp. You may need to move the potatoes round a little to get them evenly cooked. But we are not after perfection here. Only supper. Turn the potatoes, they may crumble a little, to cook the other side. They should take about ten to fifteen minutes, but will need a careful eye to ensure they do not burn. Keep the fire quite low; the butter should just bubble gently. Drain on kitchen paper and serve scattered with salt.

Slow-fried potatoes

But I also like them fried slowly, so that rather than sporting a crisp crust they become melting and tender. You could bake them, too, but the smell is more teasing when you cook them on top of the stove. You can layer them, cut thinly, with robust, punchy herbs such as thyme, and even with melting cheese, perhaps Taleggio or fontina.

Pan-fried potatoes with fontina and herbs or any other cheese for that matter

For 4 as a side dish
3 large (but not enormous) potatoes or 750g smaller ones
2 tablespoons olive oil
75g butter
a small palmful of thyme leaves
100g fontina, Gruyère or other easy melting cheese (in desperation you could use Edam)

Wash the potatoes and slice them thinly. As thinly as you can be bothered to. Put the oil and the butter in a wide, heavy-bottomed, shallow pan over a medium heat. When the butter has melted and the oil is starting to bubble, gently add the potato slices, in layers, seasoning with salt and pepper and the thyme leaves as you go.

Cover with a lid and cook over a medium heat until the potato slices are tender. Truly tender. They must be melting. You should allow about forty minutes. I know that seems a long time but it will soon pass. The heat should be really quite low.

When the potatoes are soft, cover with the cheese, which you have first thinly sliced. Replace the lid and cook till the cheese has melted. A matter of five minutes. It will ooze and slide in between the layers of potato. Serve immediately, scooping up some of the slightly golden slices and thyme butter at the bottom.

Pan-fried potatoes with browned onions and garam masala

For 2 as an accompaniment
4 medium-sized potatoes
3 tablespoons vegetable oil
a small onion, thinly sliced
a teaspoonful of garam masala

Bring the potatoes to the boil in enough cold water to cover them. Turn them down to an enthusiastic bubble and leave to cook until tender to the point of a knife – about fifteen minutes, depending on their size. Drain and peel off their skin.

Heat the oil in a pan (you might as well use the same one), then add the sliced onion. Cook over a moderate heat until a rich brown. Perhaps darker than you might normally take. Its flavour will be deeper and more aromatic. Add the garam masala and about a teaspoonful of salt. Warm gently in the pan for a few seconds until it is fragrant. Brown onions and garam masala is a most magical combination. Break the potatoes up into chunks (you can slice them but you will lose the lovely rough, crumbly texture of the dish), then stir them briefly with the spiced onion. Cook for a minute or two. Serve hot.

Chips, frîtes, call them what you will

For 2 generously
4 large, floury potatoes
dripping, lard or oil for deep-
    frying

Peel the potatoes. Cut them into long, thick slices, about 1cm in width. Put them into a bowl of cold water. This will stop them sticking together. Put the fat on to heat over a low flame. Enough to fill a deep chip pan. Bring it slowly up to 150°C/300°F. If you don't have a thermometer, then check it by adding a chip to the oil – if the chip sinks then the oil is not hot enough. If it floats in a mass of bubbles then the temperature is high enough.

Drain the potatoes and dry them on a clean tea towel. Put them in a frying basket and lower them gently into the fat. They should crackle and bubble vigorously. Fry them for about five minutes, until they are soft but still pale. Lift out and drain. Now bring the oil up to 185°C/360°F. Return the potatoes to the fat. Leave them to cook for 3–4 minutes, shaking the basket from time to time to help the chips brown evenly.

When they are golden and crisp, lift the chips out of the fat and drain briefly on kitchen paper before salting and serving.

Roast

Crisp, gooey, sticky, melting, golden and crusty – the roast potato is the crowning glory of the Sunday lunch. I have no doubt that the flavour is better when the potatoes are cooked around the roast. The spud soaks up the meat's escaped juices as it roasts. Once the joint is removed the heat can be turned up to cook the potatoes to a crisp. But you don't always have a roast in the oven.

Many cooks boil their potatoes before roasting them. A fiddle. But such a method does ensure lovely, old-fashioned, crusty edges. The gooey, slightly carbonised and crisp roast potato of our dreams.

It is the rough, crumbly edges of a boiled potato that give such a crusty result when roasted. Easily achieved by shaking the pan after the cooked potatoes have been drained, so the edges will roughen and fray. But the best one of all is the one stuck to the side of the roasting tin, the seriously fatty, crusty, gungy one.

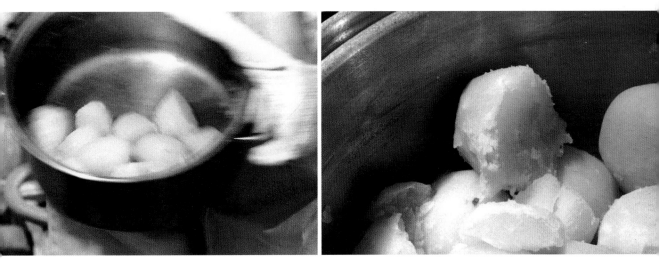

Roast potatoes

Enough for 4

900g (about 5) large, floury potatoes, such as King Edwards

lard, dripping or fat from the roast

Crisp outside, melting in.

Peel the potatoes. I would love to suggest that you don't have to but they will develop the hide of a rhinoceros. Cut them into a comfortable size (you know how big you like your roast potatoes to be), but not too small. Put them in a saucepan of cold water and bring them to the boil. Add salt, a teaspoon or so, and turn down to a simmer. The water should be at a rolling boil. Give them a good five minutes, probably a bit longer, until they are slightly soft around the edges.

Drain the water off, then return the pan to the heat. Shake the pan so that the edges of the potatoes are slightly scuffed. This will give them wonderfully crunchy, frilly edges. Tip the potatoes into a shallow metal pan in which you have heated the fat, be it lard, dripping or even olive oil. Roll the spuds in the fat, then bake in a preheated oven at 200°C/400°F/Gas 6 until thoroughly golden and crisp. A good forty-five minutes, maybe longer. Move them only once or twice during cooking, otherwise the edges will not crisp and brown.

Tip off any extra fat, sprinkle the potatoes with salt and return them to the oven for a few minutes longer till they are golden brown and crisp. Eat while hot, though it has to be said they are pretty good eaten when almost cold, or even prised away from the roasting tin the next day.

Spiced roast potatoes

For 2 as an accompaniment

3 medium-sized potatoes such as King Edwards

a knob of butter as big as a walnut

a little groundnut oil

a tablespoon of curry powder, mild or hot

a palmful of chopped mint leaves

Wipe the potatoes, but do not bother to peel them. Cut them into small cubes, about the size of liquorice allsorts. Melt the butter in a roasting tin and add a few glugs of oil to stop it burning. Add the curry powder and stir over a gentle heat until the mixture smells spicy and buttery, just a couple of minutes. Drop in the potatoes and cook over the heat for five minutes, shaking the pan from time to time and making sure the spiced butter does not burn.

Transfer to a hot oven (200°C/400°F/Gas 6) and roast for twenty-five minutes. Pour off any oil, then return to the oven, this time on the top shelf, for a further five minutes or so until the potatoes are crisp around the edges. Scatter over the chopped mint and serve.

Roast potatoes with whole garlic cloves

For 2–4 as an accompaniment
3 large potatoes, peeled
olive oil
8 cloves of garlic

Cut the potatoes into large, bite-sized lumps. Cook them in a deepish pan of salted water until they are quite tender. Expect them to take about fifteen to twenty minutes. Drain and set aside.

Heat a little oil, just enough to make a puddle in the bottom of a roasting tin. You might as well do this in the oven (200°C/400°F/Gas 6), as you will need it on anyway. Put the drained potatoes into the oil and shake the tin to coat them. Season with salt and a little black pepper – quite finely ground. Squash the garlic a little, or at least bash it about a bit. Throw it in with the potatoes.

Roast the potatoes, moving them around the pan once or twice during cooking. But not so often that they don't get the chance to go brown and crisp on each side. After about three-quarters of an hour the potatoes should be crunchy and gooey, and perfumed with garlic.

Roast balsamic potatoes

For 4
3 large potatoes, peeled
olive oil
2 large onions, each cut into 8
   wedges
thyme, a palmful of fresh leaves
   or half as much dried
3 tablespoons balsamic vinegar

Salty, savoury, crispy potatoes for eating with a roast.

Cut the potatoes into chunks, the size you like your roast potatoes to be. Pour a little olive oil into a roasting tin, enough to cover the bottom. Put the tin over the heat and add the potatoes and the onions. Cook until the vegetables just start to turn golden on the edges, then shake and turn to colour the other sides.

Scatter with thyme and a little salt, then place in a hot oven set at 200°C/400°F/Gas 6. Roast for about thirty minutes, then add the vinegar and return to the oven for a further thirty minutes. The spuds are ready when they are golden brown and crusty.

Mash

Proper mash, fluffy, golden, buttery, soothing, comforting, warming and friendly, is the food of the gods to me. It is not difficult to get right, but there are a couple of tricks I would like to pass on to you. Proper mash can only be made with a big floury potato – King Edward, perhaps, or Maris Piper. A waxy-fleshed potato will give you heavy mash. All you need is spuds and butter, and milk if you wish – it will give a lighter result. Forget olive oil and cream and all that fancy chef's stuff. Spuds and butter – that's all.

It is essential to keep the flesh of the potato dry. Dry spuds make good mash. Wet ones will give you slush. Keep the skins on and the water out. Then only the heat, and not the cooking water, will penetrate. Peeling a potato after cooking is a doddle – the skin literally slides off. Don a pair of rubber gloves and the job is done in seconds. Unless you are making mash for forty. Then squash the flesh with butter with a fork or potato masher. Both work. The latter involving considerably less elbow grease.

Buttery, fluffy mashed potato

For 4

900g floury potatoes such as King Edwards

100g butter

100ml hot milk – not essential but gives a fluffier mash

Of course, you can peel the potatoes before you mash them but it is easy enough to slip the skins off the hot, cooked spuds. You will find the mash better for it. This is a particularly buttery version of basic mash.

Rinse the potatoes, put them in a large pan of cold water and bring up to the boil. Salt generously and partially cover with a lid. Simmer until the potatoes are tender to the point of a knife, then drain them. Pull off the skins – they should peel away easily. You can wear rubber gloves if you like, or struggle with an oven glove. The best way not to burn yourself is either to hold the hot spuds in a tea towel or to be brave and hold them as best you can in your bare hands. I hold them in my hands and tell myself a little pain is good for me.

Throw the hot, peeled potatoes back into the pan and return them to the heat. Hold them briefly over the heat to dry off completely and become even fluffier. Mash them with the butter using a metal potato masher. There should be no lumps. Pour in the milk, which should be hot rather than boiling, though it does not really matter, and beat the mixture with a wooden spoon till it is fluffy and light. You might want to add more salt at this point. One must work quickly if the mash is to be hot. And it must be hot, and buttery, gloriously buttery.

You can do worse things than embellish your golden, fluffy mash with other good things. The best known is cabbage, to make a dish that glories in the name of bubble and squeak. Cooked and chopped, the green-flecked mixture is then fried till crisp on the outside. There are other good things too; cheese (a melting variety such as Camembert, fontina or Cantal, although Cheddar will work too), or bacon (fried till crisp, its hot liquid fat beaten into the mash), or cream and handfuls of herbs (parsley, lots of it and spring onions are extraordinarily good). Fried onions, too, golden and sticky, stirred into the mashed potato with a little of their cooking oil.

Mashed potato cakes with bacon and thyme

If the potatoes are thin-skinned there is no need to peel them – the skin will break into tiny pieces when you mash. If they are thick-skinned old things then you had better peel them. The skin will only get stuck in your teeth. Boil the potatoes, halved and quartered if they are very big, in salted water till tender – about twenty minutes.

Meanwhile, cook the chopped onion in a little butter and oil. You should just cover the bottom of a frying pan with oil, add a knob of butter the size of a walnut in its shell and cook the onion till it is soft, golden and tinged lightly with brown. It should smell sweet and rich. Drain and mash the spuds with a good thick slice of butter – the amount is pretty much up to you, but don't make them too wet. Stir in the onion, then fry the bacon bits in the onion pan. When they smell good, the fat sizzling and golden, add the thyme, toss it in the fat and tip the whole lot into the mash.

Season with black pepper, then leave for fifteen minutes to cool. Gently, and with floured hands, shape into eight patties. Don't be too neat; they should have a rustic, friendly look to them. Pour a little oil into the frying pan, just enough to cover the bottom, and add a small knob of butter. Heat it till it starts to sizzle, then put in four of the potato cakes. Cook for three or four minutes on each side. They should develop a thin, crisp, golden-brown crust. Don't move them round too much or they will break.

Serve hot, straight from the pan, with lots of frozen peas and, if you fancy, the salsa verde on page 37.

For 2–3
4 medium-to-large floury potatoes
a large onion, roughly chopped
butter and olive oil
a good handful (about 100g)
    bacon, chopped
thyme, a palmful of fresh or dried
    leaves

Cheese, Snacks & Puddings

Much of what we eat is not actually a meal at all. The snacks that we throw together without thought are often some of the most interesting things of all. They are certainly the most enjoyable. No doubt partially because we are impressed with our own ingenuity and partly because they are consumed in moments of hunger.

This is the food we raid the fridge for; the food that we eat on the run, standing up, or munch from the hand. No ceremony. No fuss. No trouble. Just something that will fill a hole. It could be a midnight feast, wolfed when sleepless or stoned. It could be a hurriedly concocted supper thrown down before we rush out, or it could simply be fuel. It is, in my experience, some of the best food we ever make. Inspired food for hungry moments.

Sometimes there just has to be a pudding. On a daily basis it might be nothing more than a piece of drippingly ripe fruit, or perhaps a dish of apples thrown in the oven to bake. More likely it will be a piece of cheese. While I would almost never serve a 'starter', I often find that people want to end their meal with something sweet – sometimes a spoonful of fruit crumble, other times a teaspoon of chocolate mousse. Then there are those who feel cheated if they are not presented with a vast plate of pie and custard.

I find that most puddings are better for a night in the fridge and eaten at about eleven o'clock the next morning, when energy starts to dip. In particular, cold blackberry and apple crumble, trifle, cold treacle sponge and cream and, of course, apple pie, when the pastry crust has gone slightly damp from the juice in the apples, and breaks softly, silently under the fork.

Buttery, cheesy, stodgy things

New potatoes, butter and cheese

Put a pan of water on to boil. Salt it. Tip in the potatoes. Boil till tender, about fifteen minutes. Stick the point of a knife in to see if they are cooked. Drain them, tip them on to a plate and smash them up with a fork and enough butter to make them into a thick, glistening slush, flecked with the yellow skins. Mash in some thinly sliced cheese such as Camembert or a handful of grated Cheddar or Lancashire, or similarly flavoursome cheese.

new potatoes
butter
cheese

Cheese mash

Tip the mashed potatoes into a shallow ovenproof dish. Level them a little without packing them too tightly. Dot small knobs of butter over the surface, cover with grated cheese (anything you have knocking around that needs using up) and bake in a hot oven till the cheese has melted and the potatoes are heated through.

leftover mashed potatoes
butter
cheese

Pan-fried potatoes

Break the potatoes up a little. The ideal is to end up with some big fat lumps with slightly crisp outsides and fluffy insides and some small bits to go crisp and deep golden. Heat enough butter to cover the bottom of a frying pan and add a few glugs from the olive oil bottle to stop it burning. When it is bubbling hot put in the potatoes, leave them be for a minute or two, then turn them gently over. Leave them to fry until they are golden and crunchy, the insides fluffy and moist. Drain them on kitchen paper, sprinkle them with salt and wolf them hot, with a jar of garlic mayonnaise for dipping them into.

leftover cooked potatoes
butter
a little oil

Cheese

Cheese is the supreme snacking ingredient. Who hasn't hacked off a chunk of cheese to kill a hunger pang? Or even scoffed the entire block in a moment of supreme, gluttonous laziness? The joy of cheese is partly how little you need to do with it in order to make a satisfying supper, snack or savoury. A lump of cheese is the best friend of the ravenous.

Hot cheese

Stick a large lump of cheese in a small ovenproof dish and bake it in a moderate oven till it oozes and melts. Scoop it mouthwards with crusty, floury bread.

Beans with melted cheese

For 2 as a snack
100g fontina, Camembert or
 Taleggio
a thick slice of butter, about 50g
350g/a couple of large handfuls
 of cooked beans

I am not suggesting that anyone soaks and cooks beans just for this; but should you have any cooked beans knocking around then this makes a simple, warming supper. As the beans are not cooked again you could also use tinned ones. And, in desperation, even the very worst sort of cheese.

Cut the cheese into small cubes and put half in a small ovenproof bowl in a low oven. Melt the butter in a shallow pan and let it turn nut brown. But don't let it burn. Pour the butter into the melted cheese. Stir in the cooked beans with the remaining cheese. Allow the cheese to melt completely, in the oven if necessary, before serving. Eat with bread and a glass of beer.

Melted Vacherin

Around Christmas the most voluptuous cheese known to mankind is in season – Vacherin Mont d'Or. It is expensive, and you will need to go to a proper fromagerie or one of the better food halls to track it down. But, for the most sublime snack in the world, such inconvenience is worth it. Wrap the Vacherin and its wooden casket in tin foil and bake it in a moderate oven until its skin cracks and the flesh oozes tantalisingly. A matter of fifteen minutes or so. Put it on the table with crusty, crackly bread and some tart, knobbly little gherkins. Pay the price, invite a friend, and don't ever tell me that food isn't as good as sex.

Cheese and fruit

Cheese and fruit are a magical combination. Even grotty supermarket cheese, the worst of its kind, becomes quite edible when paired with an apple. But we can do better than that. Try blue cheese such as Stilton, Beenleigh or Cashel Blue with a ripe fig or peach. Salty, juicy little snack that. Or a piquant little goat's cheese, white as chalk, with a handful of cherries or strawberries. Feta with honey-sweet melon, a craggy lump of Parmesan with a luscious pear, or the blissful marriage of a rough-skinned russet apple and a lump of deep yellow Cheddar. Or Cheshire, or Cotherstone, or Lancashire . . .

Crisp, buttery, toasted things

Garlic croûtons

white bread
garlic
olive oil

Get the oven hot to 190°C/375°F/Gas 5. Cut the white bread into thick slices, about as fat as your finger, then into cubes. Crush the garlic and mix with the olive oil. Chuck in the bread and toss it around in the oil. Put the wet bread cubes on a baking sheet and bake in the hot oven until golden, shaking them around once or twice. It will take all of ten minutes. Drain on kitchen paper, otherwise they will go soggy on you. Grind over some salt, and eat while they are hot and crisp. Of course they can be tossed with salad leaves or thrown over soft vegetables such as sautéed spinach.

Garlic bread

garlic, young, plump and fresh
butter
a lemon
parsley, quite finely chopped
bread, a baguette is best

Squash the garlic with the flat of a knife blade, or with your fist. Tease out the flesh and mash it with a little salt, using a knife blade. Mix this fragrant slush with the butter. You will need one big, juicy clove of garlic for each ounce of butter, which is easier to remember than one per thirty grams. Squeeze in a little lemon juice and add a handful of chopped parsley, not too much – just enough that it is nicely flecked with green. Cut a baguette into thick slices without cutting right through. Spread each slice with the butter, pushing it down into the slits. Bake in a hot oven, wrapped loosely in foil, till the butter is melted and the bread hot enough to burn your buttery, garlicky fingers.

Parmesan toast

a thin loaf of bread – ciabatta, baguette etc.
butter
grated Parmesan cheese

Split the bread horizontally to give two flattish pieces. Like thick slices of toast. Splitting the loaf by hand will give a rough surface which is more interesting to eat than a flat, knife-cut surface. Spread lavishly with butter, sprinkle thickly with grated Parmesan. Grill till the cheese melts and the toast drips with butter. The bread should be golden in patches. Wolf immediately.

Parmesan bruschetta

thick slices of pain de campagne or sourdough bread
garlic, peeled and halved
balsamic vinegar
thick, fruity olive oil
Parmesan cheese, shaved thinly with a vegetable peeler

Toast the bread until golden brown. While it is hot, rub the cut side of the garlic cloves over the toast so that the juice adds a faint waft of garlic, nothing more. Drizzle a little balsamic vinegar and olive oil over the warm toast and cover with a few shavings of Parmesan.

Toasted tomatoes with anchovies

bread, thick slices from a crusty loaf (sourdough would be good)
ripe tomatoes
anchovies
olive oil, rich and fruity
vinegar
(some basil or chopped parsley wouldn't go amiss if you have some)

Toast the bread lightly on both sides. Slice the tomatoes in half horizontally and put them on top of the toast, cut-sides up. Put under a hot grill till they singe at the edges, a matter of a minute or two. Meanwhile, crush the anchovies with a fork and mix in a little olive oil, vinegar, salt and black pepper, as if you are making a dressing. Drizzle over the hot tomatoes and eat straight away.

Prosciutto and melted cheese on ciabatta

Split the ciabatta in half lengthways; tearing rather than slicing will give a texture that is more interesting to eat. Toast the cut side till pale golden, the crumb still chewy. Lay several slices of prosciutto on top, then cover with thin slices of cheese. Return to the grill until the cheese melts, removing it from the heat once the cheese has become molten. Eat at once.

a small ciabatta loaf
prosciutto, thinly sliced
fontina, Taleggio or other good
   melting cheese

Melted Camembert on sourdough

Toast both sides of the bread till golden. Slice the Camembert thinly and pile on one side of each piece of toast. Zap under a hot grill till the cheese has just turned liquid and the edges of the toast catch a little. The marriage of slightly burned toast and molten cheese is one of life's great pleasures.

thin slices of sourdough bread
   such as Poilâne or pain de
   campagne
Camembert

Savoury onions, crusty bread

large onions
butter
red wine
Parmesan cheese, grated

Peel the onions and slice them about as thick as your little finger. Put them in a thick-bottomed pan with plenty of butter and allow them to cook slowly over a low to moderate heat. You can throw in some salt and pepper and a bay leaf or two if you wish. Let them stew in the butter, shaking the pan from time to time, until the onions are golden, translucent and meltingly tender. It will take all of half an hour. Pour in a few glugs of red wine. Turn the heat up, allow some of the moisture to boil away and the onions to catch here and there. Throw in a generous scattering of grated Parmesan cheese and serve hot from the pan as the cheese melts, with crusty bread. Red wine or beer to drink.

Mushrooms on toast

Fry handfuls of assorted mushrooms, cut into bite-sized pieces if needs be, in butter till sticky and golden. Season with chopped parsley, lemon juice and salt and pepper and tip while sizzling over rounds of hot toast.

assorted mushrooms
butter
chopped parsley
lemon juice
hot toast

And a couple of other good things to find in the fridge . . .

Sausage

A cold cooked sausage looks so lonely on its plate in the fridge. Yet finding one waiting for you on your return from the pub is a joy indeed. Just prise it off the plate, scrape off the fat, and stick it, bite by bite, into the mustard jar. Or, of course, you can put it in a salad. Actually it is at its most glorious with a few potatoes, so if you happen to have a squirrel store of cooked potatoes then you have treasure. Slice the sausage thickly, then toss it with the cooked potatoes and a dose of vinaigrette. Chopped parsley will perk the whole thing up. Oh, and you'll need some mustard in the dressing.

Gravy

A jug of gravy is one of the better things to come across at the back of the fridge. Two or three days old, it will taste even better than when you put it in there. Though I am obliged to say that you should treat such leftovers with care, boiling it up thoroughly and knowing its date of entry. An instant sauce for all manner of goodies – pasta, stir-fried dark green leaves, Savoy cabbage, spinach and the like – or for pouring over mashed potato or chips. Best of all is to fry some cooked potatoes in butter till they are golden and crisp around the edges and starting to crumble apart, then eating them with a pool of steaming hot gravy. Mash the crisp spuds into the hot gravy with your fork.

'Cold cuts' salads and the ultimate sandwich

Some of the most enjoyable snacks I have ever had have been made from what remains after the roast has been eaten: meat and its jelly pulled from the bones of the cold roast, flakes of cooked fish and odds and sods that didn't quite get eaten on the day.

Roast pork

Its sweet fat seasoned with plenty of salt, with fistfuls of bottle-green watercress and hunks of fruit – oranges, grapefruit or, in season, sweet and juicy plums.

Roast chicken

Pieces of the bird and its skin generously salted, tossed with chunks of melon and handfuls of crisp and perky Cos lettuce. Dress with bog-standard vinaigrette with a spoonful of honey and, if you have it, some chopped parsley.

Baked or braised gammon

A thoroughly good thing to have left over, cold ham or gammon makes a great addition to a bowl of salad. Chunks of ham, not too cold from the fridge, can be thrown in with vinaigrette and lots of chopped parsley to handfuls of shredded white cabbage in winter or broad beans and sweet onions in summer. A little mustard in the dressing, and some grapes or slices of orange, will help you forget you are eating leftovers.

Roast beef

With cold beef to use up I would usually eat it thinly sliced with pickled cabbage, frying up what was left of the potatoes to eat with it. But small pieces, provided they are still rare and juicy, would be worth throwing into a salad of mixed salad leaves, baby spinach leaves and a piquant pickle or two. Pickled onions or gherkins would make it sing. The dressing could have a bit of horseradish or mustard in it. Fried croûtons, if you have ten minutes to spare, will add welcome crunch to the pink and tender beef.

Baked fish

A lovely leftover. Whatever the variety of fish, break it into large, juicy hunks rather than mean little pieces. Whether it is salmon, cod or something a little more exotic, you can do no wrong by tossing it gently with some baby salad leaves (buy them ready washed in a packet) and some lightly cooked green beans. Keep the dressing simple, say oil, vinegar and a little cream.

The ultimate chicken sandwich

Cut the neatest slices you can from the chicken, pulling off any juicy bits and breaking them into bite-size chunks and shreds. The bread should not be so thin as to make the sandwich an elegant thing. Toast the bread on both sides, but lightly. Spread one side of each piece with mayonnaise. Be generous. Be very generous. Put several sprigs of watercress on top of one piece and some slices of tomato. Season the tomato with a little black pepper. Now cover with the chicken, which you should salt with generosity. Lay a few slices of bacon, crisp and hot, on top of the chicken. A few more sprigs of watercress, then the other piece of toast, mayo-side down. Eat.

chicken
soft white or sourdough bread
mayonnaise
watercress
tomato
grilled bacon

Fig, honey and mascarpone tart – the pastry

Enough for an 25cm tart
225g plain flour
125g fridge-cold butter
90g sugar
2 egg yolks

A rich pastry, easy to make, but slightly tricky to handle. Keep your hands cool and handle the dough as little as possible and you shouldn't go wrong.

Put the flour in a large mixing bowl. You can sieve it but it makes less difference than you have been led to believe. Cut the butter into small chunks and tip into the flour. Rub the butter between your thumbs and fingertips until the mixture looks like breadcrumbs, stir in the sugar and drop in the two egg yolks.

Using a table knife or your hands, mix in the eggs. Then use your hands again to bring the whole lot together. You may need a few drops of water but add them carefully. You should end up with a soft ball of dough. Cover with a piece of greaseproof, foil or clingfilm and refrigerate for about an hour.

Roll the pastry out on a lightly floured board so that it is large enough to fit a deep 25cm diameter metal tart tin. Lift the pastry up with the help of a rolling pin and drape it over the tart tin. Gently push the pastry into the corners of the tin and up the sides, patching any holes and tears where necessary. No one will ever know. Now turn the page.

Fig, honey and mascarpone tart — the filling

For 6

the sweet pastry case from page
   266
10–12 figs
2 tablespoons honey
6 tablespoons mascarpone
   cheese
150g crème fraîche
2 large egg yolks
4 tablespoons caster sugar

Prick the pastry case all over with a fork, place a piece of greaseproof paper on top of the pastry, and weight it down with something like beans or rice. Rest the pastry in the fridge while the oven gets to 180°C/350°F/Gas 4. Cut a deep cross in the top of each fig.

Bake the tart case for about twenty-five minutes until it is firm and somewhat dry to the touch. It should be the colour of a custard cream. Remove the greaseproof paper and beans. (This is the bit where the greaseproof paper tears and the beans go everywhere.) Leave the pastry to cool a little, then place the figs in it snugly, squeezing each one as you do so to open it up.

Stuff little spoonfuls of mascarpone into the open figs. Drizzle with honey. Mix the crème fraîche with the egg yolks and sugar and pour over the fruit. Bake for 35 minutes until the edges of the pastry have browned slightly and the juices have combined with the creamy bits to give a sort of wobbly custard. Leave to cool and set slightly for fifteen minutes before eating.

Banana tarts

Makes 4

225g chilled ready-made puff
    pastry
4 bananas
a little melted butter
a little caster sugar (say,
    2 tablespoons)
4 tablespoons apricot jam

Thin, flaky tartlets – one per person – that can also be made with sliced peaches, apricots or apples.

Roll the puff pastry out into a large square about 28cm on each side. Using a plate or bowl as a guide, cut four 13cm circles of pastry. Transfer them to a baking sheet and put them in the fridge for twenty minutes.

Remove the pastry. Preheat the oven to 200°C/400°F/Gas 6. Peel the bananas. Slice each one into rounds about twice as thick as a pound coin. Divide the bananas between the pastry, overlapping the slices where necessary. They can be higgledy-piggledy if you like. Brush them, and the pastry edges, with a little melted butter and sprinkle with sugar. Bake in the preheated oven for about ten minutes until the pastry has puffed up and the bananas are soft.

Spread the apricot jam over the tarts and return to the oven for a further couple of minutes until they are sticky and bubbling. Eat warm with vanilla ice cream.

Saint Émilion au chocolat

Enough for at least 8

200g dark, fine chocolate
225ml milk
100g butter
100g caster sugar
a large egg yolk
150g almond macaroons or
    ratafia biscuits
brandy

A rich marriage of chocolate mousse and almond macaroons that Elizabeth David first wrote about in the 1950s. It was all the rage a few years ago, though many would now declare it out of fashion. Who gives a toss? It is wonderful, especially when eaten with a teaspoon in small amounts, perhaps from an espresso cup. You should make it the day before.

Break the chocolate into pieces and let it melt in the milk in a small pan over a moderate heat. It will go thick and creamy when you stir it. Do not let it come to the boil.

Beat the butter and sugar in a basin till light and fluffy. An electric beater will make the job much easier. Beat in the egg yolk. Mix in the chocolate milk. Put half of the macaroons, crumbled up a bit, in the bottom of a china dish. Sprinkle with enough brandy to dampen them. Pour over half of the chocolate stuff. Add the rest of the crumbled macaroons, a little more brandy, then the rest of the chocolate. Leave to set overnight in the fridge.

Lemon surprise pudding

Another classic pudding that I feel has got lost. Originally from Margaret Costa's *Four Seasons Cookery Book* (Grub Street), it is one of those puddings that I just never tire of. A simple enough mixture that cleverly separates in the oven into two layers: one of sponge and the other of mouth-puckering lemon custard. It is, by the way, jolly good cold, too.

Butter a large (2 litre) ovenproof dish and preheat the oven to 180°C/350°F/Gas 4. Using an electric or hand-held beater, cream the butter with the sugar until it is creamy, white and fluffy. Add the lemon zest and juice; the mixture will probably curdle at this point but ignore it and beat in the egg yolks, one at a time. Then gently beat in the flour and the milk. You will have a dodgy-looking batter.

With a clean whisk, beat the egg whites till they stand in snowy peaks, then fold gently into the mixture. Pour into the buttered dish, then set the dish in a roasting tin with enough water in to come halfway up the sides of the dish. Bake for forty-five to fifty minutes, until the sponge has risen and a thick, lemony custard has appeared under it. Serve with cream if you wish.

For 6

100g butter
175g caster sugar
finely grated zest of 2 and juice of
    3 lemons
4 eggs, separated
50g plain flour
500ml milk

Bottom-crust fruit pie

For 6

200g plain flour

125g butter or, better still, 45g
    each butter and lard

800g fruit (yellow, red or dark
    purple plums, damsons,
    gooseberries, blackberries,
    apples etc.)

75–90g sugar

a little milk or egg white for
    glazing, and a bit more sugar

A classic American-style fruit pie with a crumbly, tatty-edged crust folded round the fruit like a big open pasty. It takes no skill. The point is to make the magical chemistry of pastry and fruit as easy as possible. Any fruit is suitable, though I have the most delicious results with plums and damsons. A lovely, crumbly, friendly pie, much easier than the recipe looks at first glance.

Make the pastry: put the flour into a bowl, cut the fat into chunks and rub them into the flour with your fingertips, lifting up handfuls of both and rubbing them between your fingers till they look like large bread-crumbs. Stir in a little cold water, about two tablespoonfuls. Bring the dough together with both hands to form a ball. It may need a little more water. The dough should be firm and not at all sticky. If it is, then add a little more flour. Try not to fiddle around with it too much, you will toughen it. Chill the pastry while you do the fruit.

Cut the plums in half and remove the stones. If you are using damsons instead you should leave the stones in. Gooseberries should be topped and tailed. Apples should be quartered, cored and sliced into bite-sized chunks.

Set the oven at 200°C/400°F/Gas 6. Take the pastry out of the fridge and roll it out into a rough circle. Use a wine bottle if you are not the sort of person who has a rolling pin. The pastry should be about 30cm in diameter. Lift it on to either a steel baking sheet, a small roasting tin or, most suitable of all, a 25cm metal pie plate. This is easiest to do if you roll the pastry round the rolling pin first, then unroll it on to the tin.

Dump the fruit in the centre of the pastry in a pile. Sprinkle with sugar. You will need more for gooseberries and damsons, less for plums and apples. Fold the edges of the pastry over the fruit as far as they will go. They will not, and should not, meet in the middle. A pie with a big hole in the middle. Brush the pastry with milk or egg white (use your fingers, it will save a brush) and scatter with more sugar. Bake for about forty minutes in the preheated oven till the pastry is golden brown, the fruit tender, and the juices from the fruit bubbling out a little.

Three-currant compote

For 4
100g blackcurrants
225g whitecurrants
225g redcurrants
4 tablespoons white sugar

Balance is important here; the ratio of red and white to black currants will affect the taste of the compote dramatically. Too many blackcurrants and its milder sisters will be lost; too many redcurrants and the compote may lack body.

Pull the currants from their stalks gently, so as not to burst their skins. Do the blackcurrants first and drop them in a heavy-based pan with the sugar and three tablespoons of water. Place over a low heat while you stalk the red and white currants.

Add the red and white currants; the mixture should simmer slowly until the juice is a rich glowing red and the blackcurrants have just started to burst their skins. The red and white currants should mostly remain whole. Taste the juice for sweetness. Add a little more sugar if you wish for a sweeter compote but take care not to overwhelm the fruit. There should be a little tartness.

Pour the compote into a bowl – a glass one will make the juices glisten. Eat warm, keeping its bright, clear flavour unsullied by cream. There will be too much for four. Eat the remainder for breakfast, stirring in a little yoghurt which will curdle luridly and startle you into consciousness.

Summer pudding – a blackcurrant version

The summer pudding, that glistening dome of bread soaked through with the sweetened juice of raspberries and redcurrants, is a celebration of the clear, bright flavour of summer currants and berries. It is a delight to make. Good though the traditional two-fruit version can be, especially if it has enough juice, the result seems somehow more interesting when blackcurrants become involved. This is not to say I approve of versions that include a mixture of 'assorted summer berries' and are inclined to taste cluttered, or anyone who suggests adding strawberries, which turn to slush and dilute the result.

The whole point is to create a balance of clear, loud-tasting fruit and delicious, juice-soaked, purple-stained, soggy bread. Blackcurrants add depth of flavour, though too many would overpower the milder redcurrants and raspberries. A small quantity, especially if they are large and sweet, somehow makes the whole pudding sing even louder. To keep the juices clear and the flavour bright, care should be taken not to overcook the currants.

Pull the currants from their stalks. If they are dusty put them in a colander and rinse them. Tip the currants into a large pan, preferably of stainless steel so that the fruit does not react with the metal. Aluminium should be avoided. Sprinkle over the sugar and bring slowly to the boil, then add the raspberries and cook until the currants start to burst, a matter of two or three minutes.

Line the base and sides of an 850ml pudding basin with thin slices of bread, leaving some for the top. It matters little in what fashion you do this, though the pieces should be as large as possible in order to support the pudding. Don't leave any gaps or a flood of juice will escape once the pudding is turned out. Spoon in the fruit, soaking the bread liberally with the juice. Fill right to the top, then cover with further slices of bread. Spoon over more juice and place the basin on a deep plate. Put a plate and a heavy weight on top. Refrigerate overnight.

Slide a palette knife between bread and basin to loosen the pudding. Turn out on to a rimmed plate; it should slide out if you put the plate on top, invert the dish and plate and give it a good shake. Spoon over any spare juice.

For 6

350g redcurrants
125g blackcurrants
150g caster sugar
350g raspberries
8 slices of white bread, any sort, cut as if for sandwiches

Plum, damson or gooseberry crumble

For 4

900g plums or damsons or 700g
　gooseberries
50g sugar, perhaps more,
　depending on the fruit
150g plain flour
100g butter
75g caster or light brown sugar

Easiest pudding in the world, and by chance one of the most delicious too. The point at which the crumble becomes utterly divine is when the juices from the fruit bubble up through the buttery topping.

Cut the plums in half and remove the stones, or remove the stalks and dried flowers from the gooseberries. If you are using damsons then you will find it easier to leave the stones in and spit them out afterwards. Put the fruit in a large, shallow baking dish. Sprinkle over as much sugar as you like, about 50–75g should be enough.

If you have a food processor, whiz the flour and butter for a few seconds until they resemble breadcrumbs, then stir in the caster or light brown sugar. Sprinkle the crumbs with a tablespoonful of water and stir through lightly with a fork. Some of the crumbs should stick together to make larger crumbs, but do not overmix; you want an uneven texture for a more interesting crumble.

No food processor? Then just rub the butter into the flour with your fingertips and stir in the sugar. Scatter the crumble loosely over the fruit, avoiding the temptation to pack it down (you want the juices to have a chance to bubble through). Bake in a preheated oven at 200°C/400°F/Gas 6 for about thirty-five minutes, until the top is crisp and golden and hopefully some of the juices have bubbled up through the crumble.

Blackcurrant or blueberry cobbler

For 6
900g blackcurrants, stalks
   removed
85g caster sugar
2 tablespoons plain flour

For the cobbler:
100g cold unsalted butter
250g plain flour
2 teaspoons baking powder
3 tablespoons caster sugar
175ml double cream

The most suitable of all treatments for blackcurrants is, to my mind, the American cobbler – where the fruit is tossed with flour and sugar which softens the flavour and thickens the juices. It is then topped with a dough not unlike that of a scone, which becomes crisp on top while absorbing some of the juices. Blueberry is the traditional cobbler fruit and, though very fine in this way, lacks the startling clout of the blackcurrant.

Preheat the oven to 200°C/400°F/Gas 6. Toss the fruit, rinsed briefly as it is inclined to be dusty if the weather has been dry, with the sugar and flour. Tip the fruit into a baking dish about 7.5cm deep and 25cm in diameter.

To make the cobbler, rub the butter into the flour and baking powder. You can do this with a food processor, though I find it easier to control it with my hands. Overmixing will result in the butter melting and making the cobbler oily. When it looks like fine breadcrumbs, stir in all but one tablespoon of the sugar and all the cream, using a fork to keep the mixture light.

Shape the dough into little patties, 5cm or so across and no more than 1cm thick. A loose and rather uneven style will appear more attractive in this instance than something symmetrical. Place the patties over the surface of the fruit. The fruit should show through in patches, the point being that its juices bubble up and bleed through the dough a little.

Sprinkle the dough lightly with the remaining sugar and bake for forty minutes till the pastry is pale gold and the fruit is bubbling. Serve with cold double cream.

Index

grilling: chicken, 80
    fish, 26

haddock: haddock fish cakes with lime leaves and
        dipping sauce, 32
    poached haddock with parsley, cream and dill, 44
ham *see* pancetta; prosciutto
herrings, 25, 42
honey, fig and mascarpone tart, 266–8

Indian bean stew with coriander cream onions, 162
Italian-style slow-cooked aromatic lamb, 128–9

Jerusalem artichokes, 234–5
    artichoke soup with garlic butter, 235
    buttered artichokes with thyme and garlic, 235
    roast artichokes, 234
John Dory, 24

kebabs: shish kebab with mint and pitta, 122
kidneys, 132
knives, 17, 19

lamb, 117–30
    braising, 126
    grilled lamb with balsamic vinegar, 123
    Italian-style slow-cooked aromatic lamb, 128–9
    lamb chops with Marsala, 120–1
    leg of lamb with garlic and rosemary, 130
    Moroccan spiced lamb shanks with aubergine,
        127
    shepherd's pie with spiced parsnip mash, 119
    shish kebab with mint and pitta, 122
    see also liver; sweetbreads
lasagne: mushroom and spinach, 223
leeks, 224
    cod, leek and parsley pie, 28–9
    grilled leeks with a gutsy dressing, 227
    shepherd's pie with spiced parsnip mash, 119
lemon: carrots with cumin and, 231
    grilled aubergines with lemon salsa verde, 215
    lemon surprise pudding, 271
    lentil soup with mushrooms and, 153
    pan-fried plaice with parsley butter and, 40
    pasta with lemon and thyme duck gravy, 92
    pasta with green herbs, toasted crumbs and, 145
    pork casserole with mustard and, 99

lemon *continued*
    prawns with lemon butter, 49
    roast fish with mint and, 34
    slow-cooked courgettes with basil and, 210
    sticky wings with, 79
lentils, 152–4
    buttered lentils, 154
    lentil soup with mushrooms and lemon, 153
    lentils with spinach and gravy, 152–3
    spiced lentils with cream and ginger, 154
lettuce: green salad, 185
    lettuce and olive oil, 186
lime: chicken noodle soup with coconut and, 151
    pan-fried Thai fish, 41
    roast chicken thighs with lime juice and ginger, 79
liver, 132
    lamb's liver with red wine vinegar and sticky
        onions, 134
lobster, 43

macaroons: Saint Émilion au chocolat, 270
mackerel, 25
    grilled mackerel with sherry vinegar, 28
marmalade: roast duck with aniseed and bitter
        orange marmalade, 90–1
Marsala: lamb chops with, 120–1
masala onion spinach, 208
mascarpone, fig and honey tart, 266–8
mayonnaise: garlic, 48
    grilled prawns and garlic mayonnaise, 49
    white bean fritters with anchovy mayonnaise, 155
meat, 97–137
    see also individual types of meat
Moroccan spiced butter: split pea soup with, 158
Moroccan spiced lamb shanks with aubergine, 127
mousses: Saint Émilion au chocolat, 270
mushrooms, 219–23
    cod, leek and parsley pie, 28–9
    lentil soup with lemon and, 153
    mushroom and onion sauté, 222
    mushroom and pine nut kibbé, 177
    mushroom and spinach lasagne, 223
    mushroom sauté, 220
    mushrooms on toast, 263
    red leaf, raw mushroom and Gruyère, 188
    slow-baked mushrooms, 222
    stir-fried greens with oyster sauce and, 208